FAMILY POVERTY

Family Poverty

Programme for the seventies

Edited by David Bull
Foreword by Peter Townsend

GERALD DUCKWORTH & CO. LTD.

Published in association with the Child Poverty Action Group

First published in 1971 by
Gerald Duckworth & Co. Ltd.
3 Henrietta Street, London, WC2

© *1971 Child Poverty Action Group*

Cloth ISBN *0 7156 0548 8*
Paper ISBN *0 7156 0593 3*

Printed in Great Britain by
Bristol Typesetting Company Limited,
Barton Manor, St. Philips, Bristol.

Contents

ABBREVIATIONS

Organisations

CPAG	Child Poverty Action Group
DEP	Department of Employment and Productivity
DHSS	Department of Health and Social Security
IEA	Institute of Economic Affairs
MSS	Ministry of Social Security
NAB	National Assistance Board
PEP	Political and Economic Planning
SBC	Supplementary Benefits Commission

Measures and Proposals

FIS	Family Income Supplement
NIT	Negative Income Tax
PAYE	Pay As You Earn
SD	Social Dividend
SET	Selective Employment Tax
VAT	Value Added Tax

Family poverty is not a subject as easy to penetrate as many people would tend to think, and we shall . . . I hope, try to understand some of the difficult interrelations and interactions which make the subject one of absorbing difficulty as well as of commanding interest.

Sir Keith Joseph
(moving the Second Reading of the
Family Income Supplements Bill,
Hansard, Vol. 806, 10 November 1970,
col. 217).

Foreword

PETER TOWNSEND

A society which is unable to comprehend, still less explain and solve, deprivation within its midst is unlikely to have much to offer the poor of West Bengal or Latin America. World and national poverty are inextricably intertwined. The forces which create and perpetuate inequality and which every week set new standards of life and of behaviour for the mass of a population operate both within and between societies. There are two general mechanisms. A system develops by which resources to live, including cash incomes but also assets, income in kind, and 'free' public services, are distributed. Resources come to be distributed unequally, for example, between regions, because of differences in natural wealth or changes in industrial demand; between communities, because of differences in communications or political integration; between classes, age groups, sexes and occupational groups, because of differences in the heaviness, skill, organisation and status of work, but also because of differences in the values which societies attach to the maintenance of a home, the rearing of children and other functions; and finally between countries, because of historical and contemporary differences of power and subjection in trading, military and political relationships. To understand why it is that some sections of a population receive so few resources we have to understand the different, and changing, parts of the mechanism of distribution.

The other general mechanism sets the national style of living. Society establishes the kind of diets people imbibe, the kind of accommodation in which they work, play and sleep, the clothing they wear and the kind of activities which they regard as natural.

There is of course considerable variety in the style of living of any population but by means of laws, regulations and social norms a partly nationwide and partly 'federal' pattern of linked community and class-styles develops. The pattern may not be clearly laid down and in nearly all societies is changing rapidly. But this is the pattern to which people are expected broadly to conform and take for granted. It is a pattern which defines the needs of a population. Those with insufficient resources to satisfy this pattern can be regarded as being in poverty.

Poverty may increase or decrease according either to a change in the distribution of resources or a change in the style of living to which a population is expected to conform. If the wages of the low-paid increase less fast than those of other groups then, other things being equal, the numbers in poverty will increase. If pensions and public assistance payments lag behind wages, poverty will again increase. Or again, poverty may increase not so much because of any change in 'differentials' as by a change in the relative amounts distributed or redistributed through inheritance or accumulation of wealth, the wage system, public social security, industrial fringe benefits and taxation.

In the United Kingdom poverty was believed for a long time after the war to have been all but eliminated. Then it was believed to be a largely 'residual' problem affecting some of the elderly, unemployed, sick and homeless. Now it is recognised as a problem which can and does affect the young family at the heart of the economic system. For the point is that standards are continuously being raised and resources being distributed in changing proportions. Paradoxically it is possible both for poverty and purchasing power to increase. There are Government decisions, such as the decisions to raise the school leaving age, introduce new legislation on the care of children and young persons, and adopt the Parker-Morris standards in housing, which increase the demands upon parents. But there are also more indirect pressures upon them, from schools, health visitors, social workers, the press and the advertising industry, to raise standards and do more for children. The pressures may be small, like those encouraging them to contribute to a school outing or buy a set of football kit, or they may be large, like those which presume they must find the space for play and homework and the time and resources to sponsor and supervise all kinds of out-of-school activities. Families are constantly reminded of the standards of which society approves and feel expected, if not always obliged, to conform to them. These standards become redefined as needs, which are psychological and social as well as physical, and which families have to fulfil. A mother bringing up children alone will often go without adequate food in order to ensure that her children are presentable at school and can mix as equals with the neighbour's children.

The problems of families in the U.K. with low incomes arise from many different sources. They are due not only to the exceptional pressures in our society to maximise opportunities for the young, raise standards of child care and establish a comfortable, labour-saving family home – which have been notable features of the post-war years. They arise from the perpetuation and perhaps worsening of low wages, the regressive nature of taxes like the flat-rate insurance contribution and the unequal system of housing subsidy and allocation. They also arise from in-built inequalities in the tax and social security systems which have been made worse by rapid inflation. For example, the allowances prescribed by Beveridge for older children were much lower, relative to other allowances, than those adopted in other industrial societies, as Margaret Wynn has effectively demonstrated in her *Family Policy*. The extension of the period at school, the derisory level and extent of educational maintenance allowances, and the failure to raise family allowances either to compensate for the withdrawal of welfare benefits *or* to match improvements in child tax allowances, quite apart from the failure to match the levels reached relative to wages in other countries, have all contributed to the relative worsening of the living standards of the low-income family. The confusion between increases to meet inflation and increases to compensate for reduction of subsidies is insufficiently appreciated. The original level of family allowances was lower than that recommended by Beveridge because it was assumed that the system of free school meals, milk and welfare foods would be extended. In fact the system was not extended. When the allowances were raised in 1952 the Government stated that this was to compensate larger families for the withdrawal of food subsidies. The annual report of the national food survey (for 1950) had shown that the subsidies represented, for example, 27 per cent of the expenditure on food of a family with four or more children but only 16 per cent of the expenditure on food of a couple without children. Again in 1968 the Government admitted that much of the increase was designed to compensate low-income families either for the effects of devaluation or for the increased price of school meals, the withdrawal of milk in secondary schools and other charges. This vital point was neglected in the government's report, of July 1971, on *Two Parent Families* and would have made their analysis of trends gloomier than it was. It would be wrong, therefore, to relate levels of family allowances only to the movement of prices or of wages. These are some of the issues which have to be disentangled in illuminating the problems of family poverty.

This book deals primarily with the kind of solutions to poverty which might be adopted in policy. What is clearer now than it was ten years or even five years ago is that to be successful any strategy must be wide-ranging – even if one measure, like increasing and extending family allowances, is given priority. Such a strategy must include an incomes policy designed to raise the lowest levels of earnings; an employment policy to reduce unemployment, particularly among middle-aged and older people who are increasingly liable to be victims of redundancy and premature retirement; a fiscal policy to reduce regressive taxes; a prices policy to submit the cost and quality of commodities bought by those on the lowest incomes to public control; a community development policy to improve the environmental conditions, housing, health and welfare facilities of poor areas, partly by extending information and legal services and wider participation in decision-making; a work situation policy to improve facilities and conditions of work and external fringe benefits; and a social security policy to introduce disability pensions, fatherless family allowances, better educational maintenance allowances, flat-rate housing allowances and national superannuation.

Certainly any strategy based on 'selective' measures aimed only at the lowest income-groups is likely, on the evidence we have, to be ineffective. Such measures are too small and peripheral in financial and institutional scale to affect more than marginally the basic distribution of resources and therefore the determinants of inequality and poverty. They do not reach many of those who are in theory eligible for them. And, paradoxically, they divide the nation in ways which actually reinforce the problems they are intended to meet. For example, different procedures come to be worked out in investigating the incomes of the poor from those which are used elsewhere to establish the incomes of the rich. A poor man who earns an extra pound on the side is treated much more severely than a business consultant who forgets to mention to the tax authorities additional fees amounting to £1,000. Separate management systems and offices are set up. The financial problems of marital separation, desertion, illness, redundancy, loss of home, accident, children starting school, job scarcity and retraining are dealt with differently from the identical problems when encountered by the rich and prosperous. Society fails to attend so closely to the principles according to which anyone, whether rich or poor, should be treated in adversity. A system of rough justice for the poor develops, certain popular prejudices about them tend to grow, and the standards by which the public may be prepared to treat people in adversity falls.

The contributors to this book give a valuable account of some of the key developments and most contentious policies discussed in recent years. They describe some of the attempts both to inform the public and educate politicians of all parties about the nature of the problem and the desirability of alternative solutions. Their function reflects the function of many organisations like the Child Poverty Action Group in recent years to help to distil and circulate information about social problems and also offer arguments about solutions for political parties to consider. It is vital that an opportunity should be afforded for such information to be circulated and policy solutions to be rehearsed publicly. As time goes on and societies grow more complex the interests of the poor and even of democracy itself can be protected only by the development of new kinds of publicity for problems, new kinds of pressure-group and new kinds of involvement of the public in decision-making.

August 1971.   Peter Townsend

Introduction

DAVID BULL

Apart from the editorial contributions, most of the essays in this collection are based on talks given to meetings of the Child Poverty Action Group (CPAG)'s Manchester and District Branch; the addresses by Sheila Kay and Tony Lynes (Chapter 2) were to a conference organised by that branch, in conjunction with the University of Manchester's Department of Extra-Mural Studies.

No attempt has been made, however, to reproduce the talks *verbatim*. In fact, David Collard was participating in a debate, while Richard Silburn developed his thoughts on community action only at the end of an illustrated talk on his St Ann's research. And although Peter Townsend delivered a talk on negative income tax (NIT), other commitments prevented him from contributing a version for publication. Fortunately, David Barker was not only able to fill this gap, but has also written a special chapter on the Family Income Supplement (FIS). Because of the confusion about 'clawback', Tony Lynes was asked to write a special chapter on this measure. Moreover, the essays have been updated where possible to relate to the situation after the 1971 Budget; and all sums of money have been translated into decimals, even when this entails such cumbersome figures as £0.41¼ for the pre-1971 standard rate of income tax (although an advantage of decimalisation is that tax rates can also be expressed as meaningful percentages).

This is not, then, an attempt to record talks given to a common audience; it endeavours to share with others that audience's good fortune. Nine experts were brought to Manchester, each to discuss a particular solution to, or strategy for tackling, family poverty. It was only as one exhilarating meeting succeeded another that it occurred to me that the speakers could be asked to contribute to a collection of essays on family poverty that would fill a gap in the literature.

There has been no shortage of pamphlets on this subject, and as a teacher, I have appreciated greatly the publication, by CPAG and the Fabian Society in particular, of literature that even the frugal student will buy; some will purchase the rather more expensive pamphlets of the Institute of Economic Affairs (IEA). I have found especially pleasing the enthusiastic purchase, by extra-mural students and those studying for diplomas in public health or municipal administration, of pamphlets on various aspects of family poverty; but one looks in vain for a comprehensive text book for *these* students. A. B. Atkinson has made an important contribution with his *Poverty in Britain and the Reform of Social Security*.[1] As he himself recognises, however, his treatment is often technical; and although he offers excellent chapters on family allowances, a minimum wage and negative income tax, his discussion of solutions to family poverty is necessarily less comprehensive than one expects of a book that is devoted, like ours, to solutions and strategies only. Indeed, we commend, to the student of this subject, Atkinson's analysis of the *problems* of family poverty and offer him here a comprehensive discussion of the main *solutions* that have been suggested to these problems, as well as two evaluations of strategies for tackling family poverty in the seventies.

Acknowledgements

Although the contributors have kindly agreed to the inclusion of their essays in a collection 'published in association with the Child Poverty Action Group', this does not signify any corporate endorsement of the views advanced in this collection : each essay represents the personal views of its author.

I am indebted to those who made possible the original talks and to the many secretaries who typed the final outcome. My main debt, however, is to the authors, especially those who had to revise their contributions in the light of the Conservative victory and consequent changes in policy. Several authors made useful comments on drafts of the editorial chapters, as did a number of colleagues in the Child Poverty Action Group. I am grateful to them all, and especially to David Barker and Tony Lynes, who not only helped to edit other essays but contributed special, additional chapters.

I owe a special debt to Peter Townsend for his foreword. We are privileged to have this contribution from a scholar who has done as much as anybody to unearth the facts, and stimulate discussion, about family poverty.

The essays

The opening chapter offers an explanation, for any readers who need it, as to why family poverty remains an issue in the 1970s. The next three chapters discuss, in the words of the first title, 'The Failure of Selectivity'; and, implicitly, in David Collard's words, 'The Case for Universality'. Although he modestly asserts that he offers no evidence that will be new to readers of *Poverty*, Tony Lynes brings together considerable material on the low uptake of means-tested benefits. He is concerned with both administrative efficiency and the dignity of the recipient. He argues that the two are 'intimately linked' (p. 27) and calls for the abolition of our 'wasteful, undignified and inefficient way of redistributing income' (p. 20).

Sheila Kay and David Collard take up these themes. 'To make a claim for help', Mrs Kay argues, 'means entering a stress situation' (p. 33). She vividly describes the humiliation, the loss of privacy and the feelings of discrimination and stigma that claimants may have to endure. Collard is more concerned with another burden that the poor must bear : 'some of the costs of "selection" are switched, *de facto*, from the general tax machine to the poor' (p. 39). He thinks it 'disgraceful that society should want to make those sections of society least able to afford it bear the costs of selectivity'.

Acknowledging such shortcomings of means-tests, some selectivists have turned to a negative income tax as a method of automatically concentrating help on those most in need. In Chapter 5, David Barker examines the pros and cons of the main NIT proposals. In the following chapter, he turns to the government's

B

latest anti-poverty scheme, the Family Income Supplement, a measure which is subject to the weaknesses of means-tests, while lacking the main advantage claimed for NIT : an automatic, 100 per cent uptake.

He shows how the case for both schemes depends on a conception of poverty as 'a remnant problem which can be solved by transferring the minimum resources to those below a line' and concludes that the debate about such schemes as FIS and NIT 'is not over means (how an agreed objective is best achieved) but over ends (how much inequality we are prepared to tolerate)' (p. 82).

Audrey Smith, in her chapter on family planning, arrives at a similar conclusion : a family planning programme has some relevance to the *alleviation* of poverty; but we must not allow the pursuit of such policies to distract us from, and obscure, the examination of the *causes* of poverty and the more fundamental policies that must follow. She is concerned, for instance, that support for the palliative of family planning might help to perpetuate the myth that large families are a major cause of family poverty. Like Sheila Kay, she draws on a number of case-studies, which she uses to illustrate a variety of attitudes that prevent the regular use of birth control.

The demands, by David Barker and Audrey Smith, for a wider view of family poverty conclude appropriately a group of six essays which review proposals that fail to comprehend the nature of the problem. The next two essays see poverty in a wider social and economic context. John Hughes emphasises that a minimum wage is no panacea : it is 'only one element in a complex economic strategy' (p. 101), which should tackle taxation, collective bargaining policy and economic management. Sir John Walley reminds us, however, of the limitations of a measure that takes no account of family responsibilities. He presents a depressing account of lost opportunities in the struggle for family allowances and regrets that once the struggle was won, family allowances were sold to the nation as part of a strategy for arresting the decline in the birthrate. He wonders whether this 'may have a lot to do with the widespread belief that family allowances promote births' (p. 110).

This is only one of the misconceptions with which Sir John deals. He devotes particular attention to the myth that family allowances are a disincentive to work and suggests that the contrary fact that higher allowances would provide an *incentive* to work should be 'the easiest way of presenting the case for family allowances in Britain' (p. 108).

Tony Lynes describes, in Chapter 10, the stages by which an attempt to meet the objection that family allowances should be concentrated on the poor was canvassed and introduced. He goes on, however, to examine the limitations of the 'clawback' device.

The next two chapters discuss different ways of pursuing an anti-poverty programme. Richard Silburn questions whether poverty lends itself to a solution through community action, while Frank Field charts the difficulties that have been experienced, since 1965, by the Child Poverty Action Group.

The concluding chapter attempts to bring together these strands of a 'Programme for the Seventies'.

1 The rediscovery of family poverty

DAVID BULL

Family poverty was rediscovered in 1965. The publication, in December of that year, by Abel-Smith and Townsend, of *The Poor and the Poorest*, was a major landmark. Their finding that poverty had been increasing during the 1950s may not have come as a surprise to those who had kept abreast of other research in this field. While previous enquiries, however, had concentrated on poverty in old age, Abel-Smith and Townsend discovered that 'of all the *persons* in the low expenditure households as many as 34.6 per cent were in households whose head was in full-time work. This is perhaps one of the most interesting and important results to emerge from the analysis'.[2]

It was an interesting and important finding because little attention had been paid, for almost thirty years, to poverty among working men: the belief in the early 1950s that poverty had been abolished had given way, over the next ten years, to a concern with a pocket of poverty among the elderly.

The early fifties: poverty abolished?

In 1950, the Labour Government went to the country, boasting that it had 'ensured full employment and fair shares of the necessities of life' and that 'destitution has been banished'.[3] These claims appeared to be vindicated when, the following year, the results were published of the third in the famous series[4] of poverty surveys in York. This revealed a reduction, since 1936, in the proportion of the working-class population in poverty, from 31.1 to 2.77 per cent; yet the level would have been 22.18 per cent in the absence of the recent welfare legislation.[5]

Few voices appear to have been raised against these findings, but Peter Townsend, researching for Political and Economic Planning (PEP), was an early dissenter. His Broadsheet of 1952 showed that there were good reasons to doubt the validity of the York findings: the dispersion of incomes in the city seemed unrepresentative of the country as a whole; nor was it clear whether the city's distribution of family sizes was representative; the sample had been drawn in a most unscientific manner; 'average amounts' had been substituted for non-respondents; and there were anomalies in the poverty standard adopted.[6] Two years later, Townsend questioned the whole approach to the measurement of poverty which the National Assistance Board (NAB) had inherited, via Beveridge, from the Rowntree tradition, with its implication that 'poor working-class people should and could live as social scientists and administrators think they should live'.[7]

When I was first introduced to the study of poverty, as an undergraduate in 1960, these two works formed the basis of our conclusion that poverty appeared not to have been abolished in post-war Britain. There was little sign yet of the welter of evidence that was to confront the student of the 1970s. There were already a few indications, however, that all was not well with the elderly.

1954 to 1965: the aged poor

As early as 1954, two official reports had drawn attention to the continuing problem of poverty in old age: an enquiry by the Ministry of Pensions and National Insurance had revealed that 54 per cent of men who chose to stay at work at 65 said that financial need was the most important reason;[8] and the Phillips Committee had shown that a number of old people 'live on or near the borderline of poverty'.[9] The evidence for the latter conclusion was twofold: the number drawing national assistance; and the results of a special analysis of Family Expenditure Survey data. The former source had, of course, been available annually for a few years, in the reports of the NAB: between

1951 and 1954, the percentage of retirement pensioner households receiving assistance had risen from 22.7 to 27.0.[10] The enquiry of 1953, however, was the first post-war survey of family expenditure; its tentative use, by the Phillips Committee, to demonstrate the relative deprivation of elderly households was an interesting departure and a step along the road that Abel-Smith and Townsend were later to take.

The Committee showed little awareness, however, of the hardship caused by a failure to apply for assistance. The fact that 'some witnesses' had told the Committee 'that there are still some old people who do not apply for assistance despite the fact that they may be eligible' was recorded without comment; and the Committee was content 'to stress that a changed attitude on the part of the public to the whole problem of national assistance is needed':[11] it must not be seen as 'simply the successor of former systems of poor relief'; after all, a state scholarship to University was 'really a form of national assistance'.[12] And although 'a few people may fail to apply for help simply through ignorance that they are eligible', the committee was 'assured, however, that it is the Board's policy to give adequate publicity to the service they provide'.[13]

Yet that same year, an enquiry was started, in Bethnal Green, into the *Family Life of Old People*. Published in 1957, the report of Townsend's classic study included a calculation that a third of the retired people in the sample had a personal income below the NAB's minimum and between a fifth and a quarter were not receiving assistance to which they were entitled. In all, three out of four had an income low enough to qualify for assistance.[14] Townsend called for 'further investigation' of findings based on his small local sample and for a recognition that 'previous ideas of "subsistence" have been wholly unrealistic'. In the next few years, a spate of enquiries and treatises was to answer both calls.

In 1962, for instance, the interim findings were published of an enquiry into the economic circumstances of 400 units in which the householder was of pensionable age. Cole and Utting concluded that 12 per cent of these households were entitled to, but not receiving, national assistance.[15] Although these findings came in for some criticism[16], they were confirmed by the Allen Report on the impact of rates[17], in 1965, and by the report of the Ministry of Pensions' own enquiry, published in 1966.[18]

By then, family poverty had been rediscovered; but in 1962, there was still little evidence of poverty in other groups. True, Peter Marris had drawn attention, in 1958, to the plight of widows when 'National Insurance . . . fell far short of protecting them against hardship and the sense of being degraded by their misfortune'.[19] And Audrey Harvey had jolted several consciences (sufficient for her pamphlet to be twice reprinted within nine months of its publication in February 1960) with her revelation of *Casualties of the Welfare State*. In a dramatic exposé of our delusion 'that we have already achieved a Welfare State', Mrs Harvey claimed that 'reluctance to apply [for National Assistance] is widespread and is by no means confined to old people'.[20] Further evidence of this reluctance was revealed, in 1962, by a Young Fabian group;[21] and earlier that year, Tony Lynes had shown how national assistance rates had failed to keep pace with the rising standard of living.[22]

The working poor

There had been little awareness, however, of poverty among the families of *working* men. Even when it was suspected that some low-paid workers were living at or below national assistance level, the lack of earnings figures related to family size prevented corroboration. Regretting this, Dorothy Wedderburn told the 1962 Conference of the British Sociological Association that income tax figures were 'useless' for this purpose: the Family Expenditure Survey would appear to offer the best prospect of evidence on this score.[23]

Addressing the same conference, Townsend described his analysis of data collected in the 1953-54 Family Expenditure Survey.[24] One household in ten was found to be living at a standard less than 40 per cent above the basic national assistance rates. Almost half were old people or couples living alone; 'but what may be surprising to some is that over a third were living in households where the head was working full-time'. Twenty-nine per cent of the people living below par were children under 16. In a footnote to his paper, Townsend revealed his tentative finding that, according to the 1960 Family Expenditure Survey, one person in seven was living below 140 per cent of the basic national assistance scale plus rent.

Similarly, Lynes thought the fact that over a third of the poor households of 1953-54 had a head in full-time work was 'one of Peter Townsend's most startling findings'.[25] He called, therefore, for an increase in family allowances and suggested that the bill could be met by cutting child tax allowances. That was in August 1963. Eighteen months later, he repeated this demand: family allowances should be more than trebled, and the pre-tax cost of £400m. 'should have precedence over income-tax allowances in allocating whatever sum the state can afford to spend on assisting the large family'.[26]

This emphasis on the large family can be accounted for by the nature of Townsend's findings: most of those poor families where the head was in full-time work had three or more children. This caused Lynes, and subsequently CPAG, in its first memorandum, to adopt a defensive position on the alleged risk that higher family allowances might cause an increase in the birth-rate.[27] Following the publication, in 1967, of the Ministry of Social Security (MSS)'s own survey, however, we could argue that almost half of the families drawing family allowances and with heads in full-time work for poverty wages had only two children.[28]

It was these tentative revelations of 1962 that were, of course, to be confirmed in *The Poor and the Poorest*. In that sense, family poverty was rediscovered three years earlier than is suggested in the opening sentence of this chapter.

Three reasons have been discussed above as to why poverty was not rediscovered sooner: an early belief that poverty had been abolished; a concentration, among those who doubted this, on poverty among the elderly and others who drew, or were entitled to draw, national assistance; and the absence of figures relating earnings to family size. This was 'an age of illusion, of missed opportunities, with Macmillan as the magician whose wonderful act kept us too long distracted from reality'.[29]

Having come back, in the mid-1960s, to reality, we entered the 1970s awaiting the results of not only a major poverty survey by Abel-Smith and Townsend, but a special official analysis of the 1968 family expenditure data. This analysis, like that made of the 1953-54 and 1960 data by Abel-Smith and Townsend, is intended to show how many families fell below the official poverty level. Ironically, the fact that the analysis was taking place was used by the outgoing Labour government to justify its failure to raise family allowances.[30]

At the same time, the Conservative Shadow Chancellor was announcing his conversion to a policy, at least in the short-term, of family allowances with 'claw-back'.[31] And in the ensuing election all three major parties mentioned, albeit obliquely in each case, proposals for family allowances.[32] This would have been inconceivable in the elections of 1964 or 1966. Since then, however, a number of proposals have been advanced as possible solutions to the rediscovered phenomenon of family poverty.

It is with such *solutions* that this book is concerned. No attempt is made to discuss further the *causes* of poverty mentioned above. The foregoing account is intended to show how evidence of poverty in the welfare state was accumulating between 1950 and 1965. It is recognised that various examinations, during this period, of the distribution of income have been omitted from the discussion. Nor was it thought necessary to offer the reader either a history of pre-war findings on the extent of poverty or a definition of this phenomenon.

These three issues have been amply covered in a variety of post-war publications.[33] The present book is intended to fill a small gap in the poverty literature, by bringing together essays on the main anti-poverty policies and strategies that have been the subject of the post-1965 debate.

2 *The failure of selectivity*

TONY LYNES

'I think I'm entitled to a school uniform grant.'
'Yes, sir, come this way, sir. Just take a seat in here and one of our officers will come and attend to you.'
'Thank you' . . .
'Good morning, sir. I believe you've come about a school uniform grant.'
'Yes. I was watching your TV commercial last night. If I've got the figures right, I think my income is just under the limit.'
'I hope you're right. According to our estimates, only about 95 per cent of people entitled to school uniform grants this year have claimed them. The District Auditor will have some awkward questions to ask if we don't find the other five per cent. Anyway, we can soon find out. Perhaps you will be kind enough to fill in your income on this form. Don't worry if you can't tell me the exact figures. Just make an estimate and we can adjust it later if necessary.'

This conversation is imaginary. It contains at least seven elements of fantasy:

1. Real people do not 'think they are entitled' to school uniform grants. They have, at most, a vague idea that the Education Department 'helps people' with the cost of school uniform.[34]

2. Real officials administering means-tested benefits do not call their clients 'sir'. Even bare politeness cannot always be relied upon.

3. Real local authorities do not advertise means-tested benefits

on television or, in most cases, anywhere else.

4. Local authority officials are seldom worried by the possibility (or even the certainty) that the benefits they are responsible for administering are failing to reach many of those entitled to them.

5. Real District Auditors ask awkward questions about improper expenditure, not about improper under-spending.

6. Applying for such a benefit in the real world generally involves, at the outset, providing precise and detailed information about one's income, under dire threats of prosecution for making a false declaration.

7. For all these and perhaps other reasons, no means-tested benefit except university students' grants[35] reaches as many as 95 per cent of those entitled to it.

Our imaginary conversation does not even represent an ideal state of things to be attained at some time in the future. A future so radically different from the present is, after all, bound to be distant. By that time, one hopes, relatively low income will not be a signal for either contempt or obsequiousness in others, and the word 'sir' will be a quaint archaism. So, one hopes, will commercial television. Long before then, moreover, the strange assortment of means-tested benefits with which the welfare state is littered will have been abolished as a wasteful, undignified and inefficient way of redistributing income. They will have been replaced – one hopes – by a far more egalitarian wage system and social security benefits based on clear criteria other than poverty. Together, these will ensure that every family in the country has an income far above the levels at which most means-tested benefits are extinguished.

Such a future demands far more than administrative changes. It demands fundamental political and economic changes and, as a by-product of them, changes in the attitudes of those who earn what they consume (or think they do) by their own labour to those who cannot do so. To predict how such changes may occur is beyond either the scope of this essay or the competence of its author. But there are smaller changes that can be brought about in the immediate future and which would go a long way towards affirming that, in principle, the rights of the poor are as important, and must be implemented as rigorously, as any other legal rights.

Evidence of under-use

It is by now generally admitted that under-use of means-tested benefits is a real problem and not merely a minor anomaly inflated by the propaganda of an irresponsible pressure group. Insofar as National Assistance (now Supplementary Benefits) is concerned, the failure of many old people to claim has been recognised since Cole and Utting published the findings of a national survey in 1962;[36] though official recognition had to await the report of a large-scale official survey published in 1966.[37] Despite strenuous efforts by the Government, in 1966, to inform old people of their rights and to encourage them to claim, a recent study by A. B. Atkinson has shown that the results achieved were disappointing, the number of non-claimants having been reduced only by about a quarter, if as much.[38]

Evidence of under-use of means-tested benefits by the families of wage-earners only began to emerge in the summer of 1966, when the Rating and Valuation Association issued figures which suggested that only half the $1\frac{1}{2}$ million householders entitled to rate rebates in England and Wales under the scheme introduced that April had so far applied for them – and only six weeks remained in which they could claim their first half-year's rebate. An intensive campaign by the Child Poverty Action Group during those six weeks resulted in a good deal of free publicity for the scheme, though it proved extraordinarily difficult to convince the Ministry of Housing that any further action was needed.[39] Official efforts to inform people of their rights had been limited in most areas to haphazard distribution of an unattractive, and in some respects misleading, leaflet; a few small posters on official notice boards; and – in the case of the more enterprising authorities – a few press advertisements. In some cases, information had been supplied to council tenants and other direct ratepayers on an individual basis, but there had been no attempt to get similar information to private tenants paying inclusive rents – the category least likely to realise that the scheme applied to them.[40]

The number of rate rebate claimants rose to about two-thirds of those entitled, and there it stuck. The Ministry continued to urge local authorities to use local means of publicity and, within the narrow limits permitted by the Treasury, national press advertising was added to the local efforts. And yet, in June 1968, the Joint Parliamentary Secretary to the Ministry, Mr Skeffington, concluded pessimistically that 'even with the publicity and all such activities . . . it is unlikely that more than one million applicants will apply'.[41] By that time, another disturbing aspect of the situation had emerged. No detailed information is available, even now, as to precisely what proportion of different categories of ratepayers entitled to rebates do not claim and why, but figures began to emerge from answers to parliamentary questions, towards the end of 1967, showing that the overwhelming majority of those applying were pensioners.[42] Very few were low wage-earners with families – the other main category entitled to rebates. These figures bore out the results of a rough calculation based on the official report, *Circumstances of Families*,[43] which showed that in June-July 1966, when about half of all those entitled to rebates had claimed them, the corresponding proportion for families with two or more children was only about 10 per cent.[44]

About the same time, evidence was beginning to emerge from official sources about the failure of low-income families with working heads to claim a variety of other means-tested benefits. Mrs Lena Jeger put an innocent-looking question to the Minister of Health in December 1966 about the number of children under five getting free welfare foods (including a free pint of milk a day), other than those in families on National Assistance. The answer given was 5,715 in November 1965.[45] Nobody knew how many were entitled but a rough estimate by CPAG suggested that the number was around 150,000.[46] This would mean that only about four per cent of those entitled to free milk and other welfare foods, other than families on Assistance, were getting them; and the fact that this estimate has never been officially refuted suggests that it is, if anything, on the high side. Subsequent parliamentary questions have revealed that, by March 1967, the numbers had fallen still further to about 4,800 *children*; while, in August 1970, 1,500 *families* were claiming.[47] Responsibility for this situation was shared between the Ministry of Health and the National Assistance Board, which acted as its agent in locating those entitled to free provision and administering the means test. It was easy enough for the NAB to ensure that

families receiving a regular assistance grant were supplied with
free milk tokens (though, even now, it is not uncommon to find
that this task has been overlooked). But the NAB had no means
of tracing the majority of low-income families with working
heads, and no wish to be burdened with the job of keeping a
constant check on their fluctuating incomes to ensure that they
were still entitled. If such families wished to apply, they immediately encountered unmistakable evidence of official apathy in
the fact that there was, until 1971, no proper application form.
It is true that bad application forms can discourage people from
applying for benefits, but even a bad form is likely to be more
effective than relying on letters or telephone calls from potential
applicants or – as was the official policy until 1971 – hoping that
it will occur to them to make use of a form intended for a quite
different purpose. With such barriers as these to be overcome,
low rates of uptake seem less surprising.

The Ministry of Social Security survey, *Circumstances of
Families*, provided further evidence, particularly on the subject
of free school meals. It is typical of the administrative muddle
surrounding benefits of this kind that free welfare foods for the
under-fives and free school meals for the over-fives are not only
administered by different authorities but are subject to means
tests which, while based broadly on the Supplementary Benefit
scale, differ in a number of important details (e.g. the allowance
made for children of different ages in the family, the amount of
disregarded earnings, and the treatment of hire purchase commitments). Thus a family qualifying for one of these benefits may
not be eligible for the other and will anyway have to go through
two separate and unco-ordinated means tests in order to obtain
them both. The survey showed that, in 1966, of the children of
fathers in full-time work who were taking school meals and
entitled to have them free, nearly two-thirds were paying for
them.[48] While this was a good deal better than the 96 per cent
failure rate for claiming free welfare milk, it was still appallingly
low. The Government's embarrassment was increased by the fact
that, as part of the price exacted by the Cabinet for the promise
of increased family allowances obtained by Miss Margaret
Herbison before resigning from the Government in 1967, the
price of school meals was to be raised, in April 1968, by 50
per cent.[49]

Action of some kind was clearly necessary. It took the form of a circular letter from the Education Minister, Mr Gordon Walker, sent to all parents of school children, reminding them of the possibility of claiming free school meals and giving the income limits. This enabled parents to work out for themselves whether they were likely to qualify, and a tear-off slip at the bottom of the letter reduced to a minimum the formalities of applying : parents could ask for further information, for an education welfare officer to call, or for an appointment at the education office. The tear-off slip was a way of getting into the pipe-line potential applicants, who might have been unable to complete, unaided, an application form. The experiment was a notable success. The number of free meals served each day rose by 100,000 in a matter of weeks. It is true that the numbers were already rising steadily, presumably as a result of the publicity given to the statistics, but there can be little doubt that the letter had a major impact. Unhappily, in the May 1970 repeat of this exercise, the tear-off reply slip was omitted.

About the same time as the Gordon Walker letter, the decision to re-introduce prescription charges was announced. A week before the announcement, CPAG published a report on the administration of refunds of other health service charges – for spectacles, dentures and dental treatment. It was the usual story of inadequate and misleading publicity and official apathy – with the usual result that, while people drawing supplementary benefit stood a reasonable chance of being told about their rights, the low-paid worker and his family were most unlikely to learn of their entitlement to free provision. Of the half-million cases in which help was given by the Ministry of Social Security towards the cost of spectacles in 1966, only about one per cent involved people who were not already drawing benefit. CPAG estimated that about five times as many were entitled to such help. A rough calculation suggested that the situation regarding prescription charges before the Labour Government abolished them tempo-rarily in 1965 was very similar.[50]

In the light of this report and the strong feelings aroused by the reintroduction of prescription charges, one might have expected the Ministry of Health to devote a good deal of care to the exemption arrangements, especially in relation to the exemption of low-paid workers. This did not happen. Indeed, publicity about the exemptions ignored the low-paid worker and his family altogether, apart from a cryptic reference to 'other people needing help to pay the charges', who were advised to obtain a form from the post office. The form in question turned out to be lamentably designed, seriously misleading (though complaints from CPAG resulted in some improvements in the second edition), and difficult, if not impossible, to obtain from many post offices.[51]

One of the most curious episodes in this saga of official ineptitude was the 'entitlement campaign' announced by the new Minister of Social Security, Mrs Judith Hart, in March 1968.[52] The intention was that fourteen million leaflets, giving information about a wide range of means-tested benefits, were to be sent, by post, to families all over the country. About 80 per cent of households were to be covered in this way, only those in relatively prosperous areas being excluded. Another two million leaflets were to be distributed to the Ministry's local offices, local authorities and voluntary bodies.[53] Mrs Hart deserves the fullest credit for launching this imaginative campaign, even if she underestimated the difficulties of providing the necessary information in a way which would encourage those eligible to apply for the benefits (in the case of benefits such as school uniform grants and education maintenance allowances, which are fixed independently by each local authority, all that a national leaflet could do was to mention their existence; no details of income limits could be given). It appears, however, that she also underestimated the reactions of some of her ministerial colleagues. Possibly in obtaining Treasury approval for the cost of printing and distributing sixteen million leaflets, she omitted to mention the additional costs resulting from increased uptake of benefits if the campaign succeeded. Or perhaps other Ministers (e.g. of Education and Housing) objected to this attempt to pre-empt part of their departmental expenditure budgets. Whatever the reason, the campaign did not commence in June 1968, as promised. Instead, it was launched with a minimum of publicity at the end of July, and the postal distribution of leaflets was confined to selected areas covering less than half the country. In her determination to do good by stealth, Mrs Hart used the same opportunity[54] to announce a series of punitive measures against the 'workshy', which naturally aroused much more interest in the

C

news media than an attempt to ameliorate the conditions of low-paid workers.

The reason given for reducing the scope of the entitlement campaign was that the first stage was to be used as a controlled experiment. The numbers claiming benefits in the areas covered would be compared with the figures for other areas to test the effectiveness of this method of publicity. Three months later, Mr Michael Barnes, MP, asked when the leaflet was to be distributed in London (one of the areas excluded from the first stage) and was told by the Minister that the results were still being assessed and that, anyway, the leaflet was now out of date.[55] After another three months of official silence, the Department of Health and Social Security informed CPAG that the campaign had not, after all, provided a means of assessing the effectiveness of different methods of distributing information. Where an increased demand for benefits had occurred, it was impossible to say whether it had resulted from the distribution of the leaflet.[56] Nothing further was heard about the extension of the campaign to areas not covered by the first stage. Nor was there any suggestion that other experiments of this kind would be undertaken. Instead, the Department's public relations activities were concentrated on the more straightforward task of reinforcing public prejudice against the unemployed. It was only when the Conservative government decided, in 1970, to embark on a new round of increased charges that Ministers felt obliged to announce another 'take-up' campaign. Originally planned to commence in March 1971, the campaign was deferred because of the postal strike. The increases were not.

Obstacles to improved administration

If the efforts made at the national level to encourage low-paid workers and their families to use the benefits to which they are entitled have been spasmodic and half-hearted, it can at least be said that the problem is recognised and that some of the Ministers concerned have shown the will if not the ability to solve it. If they have failed, it is in part because, without a major effort to rationalise and co-ordinate the various benefits and means tests, efficient administration is impossible; and since rationalisation inevitably means making some of the conditions for claiming benefits more generous, pressures on public expenditure in recent years have not encouraged this kind of exercise.

At the local level, however, there is less sign of change. With rare exceptions, local authorities continue to administer astonishing numbers of differing means tests, with little effort to rationalise or co-ordinate them either between neighbouring authorities or within the same authority. Publicity is generally minimal and it is still common to find local government officials deliberately attempting to conceal the precise conditions for claiming benefits (even those like free school dinners which are the subject of central government regulations), on the grounds that publicising such details would encourage fraudulent claims.

It is difficult to see any real justification for continuing to leave the administration of a variety of means-tested benefits in the hands of a number of different local authority departments. It is even more difficult to believe that any useful purpose is served by allowing each authority to fix its own rates of benefit and income limits for such benefits as school uniform grants, rent rebates and – least defensible of all – education maintenance allowances, which could and should be one of the most positive measures for reducing inequalities of educational opportunity based on income. If university students' grants are paid on a single nationally applicable scale, why should these allowances to enable children over 15 to remain at school be subject to the whims (and, all too often, the neglect) of individual education authorities?[57]

I have not attempted, in this essay, to offer a precise definition[58] of such terms as 'rights' and 'entitlement' in relation to the field of welfare benefits. Nor have I offered any new evidence; readers of the CPAG quarterly journal, *Poverty*, will be familiar with all the material presented here. It seemed worthwhile, however, to bring together some of the evidence that has emerged from the experience of the past four years, which at least tells us something, negatively and by implication, about the consequences of enacting and administering benefits without adequate concern for either the efficiency of the system or the dignity of the recipients. Not the least important lesson to be learned from this experience is that these two objectives – efficiency and dignity – are intimately linked. Whether either is attainable in a system are intimately linked. Whether either is attainable in a system of means-tested benefits, entitlement to which depends on proof of poverty, is a question that cannot yet be answered with certainty. At this stage, there is much room for experiment but no grounds for optimism.

3 Problems of accepting means-tested benefits*

SHEILA KAY

Stigma not only affects those with a problem, who have to live with the feeling of being shameful or different, but it acts as a warning to others who might have the problem but narrowly escape, or hide the fact. It also affects the reactions of other people towards the stigmatised. The older terms – pauper, criminal, lunatic, prostitute; the modern terms – layabout, juvenile delinquent, ex-mental patient, unmarried mother and coloured immigrant, call up a series of stereotypes of irresponsible people lacking in the accepted standards, collectively different and to be treated with suspicion and reserve, and in particular, having their right to maintenance in financial need, sickness or unemployment put under a microscope.

The effect of stigma

Fear of being 'branded' in this way involves those in need of help in a range of emotional reactions, from shame and refusal to apply, through confusion about requirements, resentment and 'hostility towards a system which deliberately and continually creates the role of suppliant',[59] through desperate efforts to tap every source, to fight or flight. The fight may be constructive, or it may be expressed in 'putting one over' on the authorities; the flight may be into apathy or, by 'doing a moonlight flit', escaping

---

* This essay draws not only on Mrs Kay's professional experience, but also on her welfare rights activities as a member of the Merseyside Child Poverty Action Group.

from rent arrears and debts. The fear may not be justified, and a sense of relief and restored self-confidence is experienced if a considerate hearing, followed by help, is given. In others who do not apply for help, their ignorance of benefits available may be the chief reason why they adapt to a restricted life and defend themselves and their children against disappointment by reducing their demands on life compared with those around them, thus giving the appearance of apathy.

In both of the Merseyside CPAG Welfare Rights projects, we have found confirmation of this consciousness of stigma again and again. In the second study, a small proportion of those who knew about the benefits said they would not claim them, even if they were eligible :

The reasons for this reluctance to apply for what are rights varied considerably, but could be divided between four groups : i) those who felt, with regard to education benefits, that their children would be jeered at if they received them; ii) those who preferred to be independent and manage somehow by themselves; iii) those who felt the 'red-tape' involved in applying was not worthwhile for the small return; iv) those who had been refused on previous applications and refused to be 'humiliated' again.[60]

In the first study,[61] there was a core group of about one-third of those in poverty who were receiving supplementary benefits and who knew about many other benefits such as free welfare foods, school meals and clothing, though not often about rent rebates. Then there was a group of working men's families – low paid labourers, drivers, etc., who knew very little of these rights and viewed their acceptance with considerable doubt; not that they were free from financial anxiety, for one docker said that only the recent strikes, giving him an increase of over £3 per week, had enabled him to look forward to rehousing with its prospect of a rent increase. A third group included a number who refused or were initially hesitant to complete the questionnaire and several who declined help in applying for benefits for which they appeared to be eligible. Many of these were retired people who 'did not discuss their business with anyone'; at least two of them were drawing £4.50 retirement pension plus £1.50 per week out of savings to pay the rent, rather than claim a supplementary pension.

One young woman refused to talk to the student who first called on her, but eventually opened the door to 'someone older' :

> After being reassured about confidentiality, she explained that she did not want her neighbours to know she was unmarried. She had two children, and was living on supplementary benefits and having some difficulties in managing, but the older girl who was at school either came home for lunch or paid for dinners. When we discussed free dinners, both she and the little girl assured me that everyone in the class had known about it when she was getting free dinners the previous year and the child could not face it again. Although I dropped the subject, I must admit I doubted that everyone knew, until some weeks later in the summer of 1968, my own child of seven volunteered that yellow tickets were for those who paid, and pink tickets were for the free dinners, at school.[62]

This is an example of stigma having a twofold effect : it was painfully disadvantageous to the child who bore it, and the knowledge of her reactions might affect her classmates' willingness to accept free meals, so that it was also a deterrent to the population at risk. The disadvantage of being in poverty and asking for help includes loss of privacy in one's private life and relationships, and in one's financial affairs, and may include loss of confidentiality about other things. Dennis Marsden, in *Mothers Alone*,[63] discusses the effect of stigma upon mothers without husbands in their homes. Not only were many of the mothers conscious that their single, divorced, deserted or widowed state led them to be regarded as 'easy meat' by male acquaintances, visiting tradesmen and callers; but 'fears of the woman's possible cohabitation caused officers [of the then National Assistance Board] to treat a large proportion of the mothers with suspicion'.

If there are grounds for such suspicions, their chances of achieving a more regular way of life were illustrated by one mother who asked advice of CPAG, and complained that she was 'always having her money stopped' although she had three children :

She was concerned that a strange visitor had called, saying he was from the Ministry of Social Security, though he 'only had a little black book and not the usual case sheets'. When she asked for identification, he laughed and said she knew very well, so she refused to answer any more questions, whereupon he referred, in front of a neighbour and the eldest child aged nine, to the fact that she had a police record. She said she was going to consult a solicitor; she was sick of being hounded for a conviction seven years ago 'when all [she] had done was stand talking to a strange man in the street'; since then she had several times been questioned by the police when she was out of doors in the evening, and an official had once met a request for a clothing grant for the children with the suggestion that she 'go out and earn it'. She existed, one felt, in an embattled relationship with the authorities who she felt drove her into the way of life she still denied, and about which she felt extremely ambivalent.

Social expectations and misunderstandings

Two of the reasons why means-tested benefits are not claimed are the loss of privacy they may entail, and their association with an unacceptable image. These reasons seem to apply particularly to those, whether working or retired, who have enough to exist on but would be better off with the additional benefits to which they are entitled. A further difficulty is that low paid workers think of such benefits as free school meals and free welfare milk as being the prerogative of supplementary benefits claimants (who must not be in full time work).[64] An estimated 96 per cent of low paid workers entitled to free welfare foods failed to claim them in 1967.[65]

People's expectations of themselves are an important factor in their actions: ordinarily, a husband and father is seen as the breadwinner; in a particular job; the head of the house; and the provider of the home; and a wife as a good mother and house-keeper, who may work 'to help out' if necessary. They have an emotional investment in these social roles and in the well-being and behaviour of their children, and self-respect depends largely on carrying out these roles adequately or having a socially accept-able reason for not doing so. Extreme difficulty may be experi-enced in adapting to change in the tragic circumstances often

surrounding pit closures or the run-down of villages like Pity
Me, in Durham, even when mobility is socially sanctioned.[66]

If people give up the right, or lose the ability, to manage by
their own efforts, not only does this self-image suffer, but when
they turn to the authorities there is often the fear of being in the
power of a mysterious 'they' who may change the rules and put
you in the wrong, may not believe what you say, and often fail
to explain why you are not entitled to benefit. A hospital cleaner
whose husband had long periods of unemployment told me of
one such occasion:

> The eldest of her seven children was at Grammar School and
> they had applied for a School Uniform Grant. When, in June
> 1968, she had gone down to collect the third instalment of the
> £24 p.a. awarded, she was informed that her circumstances
> had changed since the award was made and she was no longer
> entitled to the final £8. She argued that her husband was still
> out of work, but was reminded of the recent increase in family
> allowances. This had been absorbed, in two instalments,[67] into
> their very limited budget but she came away empty-handed,
> after giving the official a piece of her mind and went home to
> try to explain to an incredulous teenager.

Here the problem seems to be one of timing an increase in
local authority scales so that the higher family allowances benefit
the family instead of appearing to save the authority money.
More rapid adaptation of local authority scales to changes in
central government benefits, whether family allowances or
supplementary benefits, would prevent this problem from arising,
but at least an effort should be made to offer an explanation to
the claimants already 'on the books' when such changes reduce
their entitlement.

Understanding the system and being organised to claim a
right to which one is eligible, fill in the forms, keep a note of
national insurance and medical numbers and previous earnings,
get confirmation of income from an employer, all demand considerable resources of energy, time and effort. These are not
always available at the time when they are needed – for instance,
in pregnancy and following the birth of a child.

To make a claim for help means entering a stress situation
in which one feels very much at a disadvantage, because it is

much more strange to the new applicant than to those who work in the office or agency, and who may take for granted things which need explaining, such as how long you have to wait, or where the nearest lavatory is. To belong to the category of unemployed or supplementary benefit claimants in an old industrial city may also reinforce recognition of oneself as being one of a certain type; there are more prepossessing, separate entrances for the professional and technical unemployed in some offices than for manual workers seeking jobs, as indeed there are in many factories; a photograph in *Poverty*, in 1967,[68] showed the public entrance at the rear of a London office of the Ministry of Social Security, flanked by six dustbins on one side and a queue of people on the other.

The feeling of being discriminated against is, for some of our city dwellers, part of their daily experience. 'You can't get a hire purchase agreement if your address is Liverpool X', it is often said; sometimes 'You can't get a good job', either. These reactions are often expressed by the coherent and active rather than the defeated and apathetic, and the community councils movement in such areas is an organised opposition to the acceptance of discrimination. Yet environmental poverty such as this, described in a report on the problems of coloured school leavers, is a challenge to make one pause :

> The standard of housing is generally low (medium and large Georgian and Victorian houses, frequently multi-let) and part of the area is gradually being 'slum-cleared'. Overcrowding is very common and cases of families living in one room are not infrequent. Maintenance generally is poor, even in the new blocks of corporation flats, and especially those without resident caretakers. There are large parks at the south end of the area, but within the area itself playing space is virtually non-existent except for the streets.[69]

One might add a mention of the great age of the primary school buildings, usual in such an area.

More militancy needed?

The feelings of frustration which arise within such situations as we have been considering, and of concern for redress which arise out of our knowledge, can result in various forms of action. The logic of the short-term solution becomes clearer when the circumstances are understood, as when a labourer rehoused with his wife and nine children found himself unable to meet an electricity bill of £29 :

> Facing a cut-off, he 'asked for his cards' and drew £31 – one week's wages plus his 'week in hand' – and after paying the bill he applied for national assistance as he was now unemployed, and was offered £6. This he regarded as an insult, and he stormed out of the office on Friday afternoon refusing it, and rang the NSPCC and the Children's Department to ask for their interventions. He retrieved his sense of dignity by doing battle – 'if they can get awkward with me, I can get awkward with them'. The result was a special message from the office telling him the money was still available, and the rejected £6 was duly collected on Saturday.

Social justice cannot allow the children of the low-paid, the sick, the unemployed and the unsupported mothers, or of the socially stigmatised area, to grow up with their experience and development restricted by poverty, almost as if they were destined to fill a future 'pool' of half a million unemployed. But a movement in the 1970s which is strong enough to achieve higher minimum wages and subsistence family allowances and other changes in social policy, thus reducing the need for means-tested benefits, will have to include both the Trade Unions and the social reformers of many shades of opinion as well as a pressure group such as CPAG. We have still to see the end of the situation, described in 1967, in the Supplementary Benefits Commission (SBC)'s White Paper on the Wage Stop. After describing the ill health, the debts, the lack of pocket money, the diet, clothing and bedding problems of the fifty-two families (many of whom were not receiving means-tested benefits such as rate rebates) in its survey, the Commission concluded :

> The general impression derived from these visits was not so much one of grinding poverty in any absolute sense as one of unrelieved dreariness with, in some cases, little hope of improvement in the future.[70]

The most important lesson the means-test has for the 1970s may be that an effective protest movement needs to be more militant; the image of CPAG as supplying information and helping people fight back to achieve better conditions can win increasing support from those in poverty. People organised in their own defence can make a basic advance towards social justice; and knowing one's rights can help to modify some of the deterrent effects of means tests.

4 The case for universal benefits

DAVID COLLARD

'Universal' benefits are more *efficient* at solving the family poverty problem than are 'selective' benefits. These terms will be defined in a moment. I am *not*, at present, concerned with the rather different issue of whether benefits should be provided publicly (by the central government or the local authority) or privately (through the market). I have already examined this question in a Fabian Tract.[71] It was there shown that the well-known defects of free markets – their dependence on an unfair distribution of income, their susceptibility to monopoly pressures and their disregard of social costs – would be present in an exaggerated form in the fields of health and education. Most of these defects would remain even if lower income groups were given 'vouchers' to supplement their incomes. I shall be concerned, instead, with publicly provided benefits in cash and in kind. The issue is whether these cash benefits should be provided universally or selectively.

Criteria of need

One encounters, in popular discussions, the rhetorical question : 'Should benefits be provided for everybody or only for those who need them?' It all depends on what you mean by 'need'. Those of us who argue for universal benefits are saying that the criterion of need should not be income but a whole set of relatively objective criteria : for example, the need for medical or dental attention, pregnancy, having children of school age, etc. That is to say, there will, for any type of benefit, be a *trigger criterion* which, if satisfied, entitles a person to that benefit regardless of income. It is immensely important that the criterion should be simple and easy to understand (as in the case of family allowances). The benefits are then financed from general taxation. Selectivists, on the other hand, argue that this is a wasteful method. They wish to impose a double criterion for free benefits : first a trigger criterion of the objective sort that I have just mentioned and, secondly, a *low income criterion*. Only those people satisfying both criteria actually get the benefit.

A selective system is defined here as efficient if the quantity of benefit received (in cash or kind) is equal to the total theoretically available, i.e. the benefit obtainable if all those who satisfy a trigger or financial criterion apply. The *marginal cost* of making a selective system more efficient is the cost of raising the efficiency ratio by one per cent and is likely to rise as efficiency rises. Thus it will be relatively easy to raise the efficiency ratio from 10 to 20 per cent but very difficult to raise it from 80 to 90 per cent.

One may distinguish between selective, universal and hybrid systems. The simplest system is a purely universal one. The only important decision to be made is whether the first trigger criterion is satisfied. Thus for pensions, we ask : 'Is the person of pensionable age?'; for education, 'Is the child of school age?'; and for invalid cars, 'Is the person disabled?'. This main trigger has nothing directly to do with income. Two things can usefully be said about it. First, information about benefits must be widely and easily available : regardless of whether benefits are universal or selective, money can usefully be spent telling people which services exist. One's general impression is that middle-class people are relatively skilled at discovering benefits. To redress the balance, one needs more use of direct advertising and greater expenditure on social workers and local information centres. The second thing to be said is that there will be an element of self-selection. I am the one who decides whether or not I need medical advice and (over a range) my choice may be arbitrary. This will only partly be due to whether a fee is involved; principally it has to do with uncertainty. At every income level there will be those who are averse to taking health risks (hypochondriacs). To minimise 'mistakes' in self-selection one must rely on

information, education, and the judgment of those who work in
the health services.

Now consider a purely selectivist system. The benefit may be in
cash or in kind. If it is to be in cash a means test will determine
whether or not it can be received, for example, clothing and
maintenance allowances for school children and maintenance
grants for university students. If it is to be in kind, there may be
fees (or charges) for everybody, with refunds for those on low
incomes, or fees except for those on low incomes. Apart from
the two pure types, there are hybrids. Exemption from charges
may be made if *either* a second trigger criterion is met *or* if the
beneficiary has a low income. Certain classes of people (pensioners, children, pregnant women) may be declared exempt. There
may be further exemptions for people receiving supplementary
benefit; but there will be no automatic exemption for households
whose breadwinner is on low pay but in employment. They must
undergo a means test. The exemptions from prescription charges,
as operated since 1968, are a good example.

The case against selectivity

Arguments against the means test (or 'low income' test) are well-
known. Essentially, there are two lines of criticism. First, there
is the humiliation, described in the previous two chapters. It
is emphatically *not* the same sort of 'test' that the middle-class
parent of a student or the prospective mortgagor experiences.
Secondly, there are complications in the means test procedure.
Mike Reddin has shown that local authorities offer a bewildering
complexity of means tests – from payments for home helps to
rent rebates.[72] This combination of humiliation and complexity
has several important implications:

1. Some of the costs of 'selection' are switched, *de facto*, from
   the general tax machine to the poor. These costs are very real
   and only some of them can be measured in money terms –
   trudging from office to office, waiting, filling in ill-understood
   forms, paying bus fares and so on (see Figure 1). It is disgraceful that society should want to make those sections of society
   least able to afford it bear the costs of selectivity.
2. The costs of claiming cash, exemption from a fee or a rebate
   may be such as to discourage claimants. When entitlements

are efficiently publicised, easy to obtain and involve no loss of face, relatively few of those entitled fail to claim; yet even in the relatively simple problem of school meals,[73] this has been difficult to achieve. Notice that the cost of increasing the ratio of those receiving a benefit to those entitled will rise more rapidly the greater the degree of success already achieved. The school meals case is a relatively easy one because children can be used as messengers to take information about free meals to *all* parents. It is much more difficult to inform low-paid workers of their entitlement to free welfare foods : the costs of making selectivity even modestly efficient in their case would be very high indeed.[74]

3. People who fail to claim an exemption from a fee or a rebate must either contract their use of the service or continue to use it at the same level. On this question, there is a fairly straightforward division between right and left. If people contract their use (e.g. of prescriptions), right-wingers see this as evidence of previous malingering and scrounging; left-wingers see it as evidence of present deprivation. If people do not contract their use but continue to pay fees at the same level of use, it must be the case that the burden of financing has passed from the taxpayer to the recipient of the benefit; i.e. the shift is a regressive one. Again, the right versus left distinction is relevant : right-wingers are not concerned about this redistribution; left-wingers are.

Can selectivity ever be justified?

The question now arises of whether there are any circumstances under which fees plus selectivity would be justified. To answer this question, we need to say a little about the over-all purpose of our system of benefits. What is it all for? Some goods are too important to be left to the free market; the state should have a frankly paternalistic attitude towards them. (Liberals are frequently ashamed to have to admit to paternalism; socialists are not quite so sensitive). The free provision of benefits in kind is egalitarian as well as paternalistic. While the whole structure of taxes (income tax, indirect taxes, national insurance contributions, etc.) is neither progressive nor regressive, it is true that benefits in cash and in kind redistribute real income in favour of lower income groups.[75] Unfortunately, the amount of redistribution is rather worse than an averaging of statistics would suggest; some working class areas have school buildings that are very inferior indeed. The role of the first trigger then becomes central – does it allocate the amount of services available fairly as between individuals? Even in education and health the answer is sometimes 'no'. We know that, particularly in education, articulate middle-class people do rather better than they should. In housing, the unfairnesses are particularly blatant. The continuing shortage of private rented accommodation has meant that people on the waiting list are badly off relatively to people in council houses (the council house tenant is not, however, well off relative to the house owner who obtains tax relief on mortgage interest).[76] This shortage produces a powerful 'equity' argument in favour of rents rather near economic levels.

For the out-and-out universalist, this poses a difficult question. It may be more just to offer council houses at near-economic rents, with rebates for the less well-off, than to charge a uniform subsidised rent to all those lucky enough to be allocated council houses. Such adjustment is necessary because of the equity problem as between council house tenants and private tenants. But it would no longer be needed either if council accommodation were available on a larger scale or if a system of housing allowances could be devised.[77] Notice that a housing allowance scheme would in no way remove the need for more local authority housing.

Similarly with rate rebates. Rates are unfair because they bear heavily on the less well-off :[78] rate rebates are a way of redressing the balance. It is more just to have rate rebates together with a means test than to have no rebates at all. Again, they would no longer be necessary *either* if a different and more equitable form of local income tax could be devised *or* if low incomes could be increased by universalist measures. These concessions to selectivity do not undermine the universalist case. Such means tests are expedients for making the best of a bad job : so long as we have such an inefficient system of housing subsidies and such an unfair form of local taxation, we must tolerate rent and rate rebates. The equity question has caused Mr Crossman recently to argue that a system of housing allowances might be fairer.[79] I suggested, in my Fabian Tract, that vouchers plus more use of the market

D

could be less harmful in housing than in education and health.[80]

The respective costs of universality and selectivity

Three sorts of cost are of interest:
  1. Transfers to persons
  2. Real resource costs
  3. Exchequer costs

These are set out in Figure I, which has been drawn up with cash benefits in mind. It is very important not to confuse these three types of cost. We have seen that transfers to persons will be lower under a selective scheme than under a universal one. What of the other costs?

It is pretty certain that real resource costs will be greater under a selective system. There is one minor respect in which they will be less: the administrative costs of actually paying out benefits will be lower. But, in two major respects, real resource costs will be higher. First, the machinery for conducting means tests will almost certainly cost more than the Inland Revenue resources theoretically 'freed' by less tax recoupment: the costs to the Inland Revenue of recovering part of, say, family allowances must be trivial. Secondly, the whole selective procedure is likely, as we have seen, to involve recipients in extra time and trouble. 'Time and trouble' costs are just as real as any other but they are not taken into account as market costs: they would, however, have to be included in a cost-benefit analysis.

Figure I
The Respective Costs of
Universal and Selective Cash Benefits

Costs Involved	Nature of Benefit	
	Universal	Selective
Transfers to Persons	Gross Cash Benefit *minus* Tax Recouped	Cash Payment
Real Resources Used	Costs of Payment *plus* Recoupment Costs *plus* Time and Trouble	Costs of Payment *plus* Means Tests Costs *plus* Time and Trouble
Cost to Exchequer	Gross Cash Benefit *minus* Tax Recouped *plus* Costs of Payment *plus* Recoupment Costs	Cash Payment *plus* Costs of Payment *plus* Means Tests Costs

Last, the design of a humane and efficient system of social benefits is bedevilled by bogus economic arguments about incentives, the burden of taxation, and balance of payments and so on and so forth. We have come to accept absurd arguments of the following kind: 'If we want more nursery schools we must cut down on sixth form colleges'; or 'If we want more hospitals we must cut down on teachers'. We have come to take it for granted that the public sector should not be expanded. We forget that the basic choice is about use of resources, whether to build office blocks or schools, to train sales executives or teachers. We lack not resources but political will.

It is odd that selectivists, who claim to attach so much importance to what the country can 'afford' in economic terms, should so easily confuse real resource costs with exchequer costs. Although politically important, exchequer costs are a bastard mixture of real resource costs (though only some of them) and of money transfers.

Conclusions

My main conclusions are:
1. The marginal cost in terms of publicity, personal contact, etc., of making selective systems 'efficient' is very high for most types of benefit.
2. In the absence of a perfectly efficient selective system the imposition of fees for benefits in kind must lead either to deprivation or to financial hardship.
3. Various types of cost must be distinguished. Real resource costs will almost certainly be higher under a selective than under an alternative universal system.

5 Negative income tax

DAVID BARKER

Since negative income tax is a relatively new idea about which there is a great deal of confusion and misunderstanding, it will be worth explaining, at the outset, what I understand by the term. It is a scheme which would probably be operated through the present PAYE structure. Income tax forms would be completed as they are at present; but instead of being used only as an assessment of the tax payable by those whose income is *above* the tax threshold, the return would also provide the basis for computing cash benefits payable to (i.e. negative taxes are 'taken' from) others whose income is *below* this level. The proportion of the gap between income and the tax-threshold which is made up can, in theory, vary from just above zero to 100 per cent. In practice, proposals vary from about 33 to 100 per cent. Take a family with an income of £10 per week whose various reliefs entitle them to a tax-free income of £15 at which point their income would become taxable. With a negative tax rate of $33\frac{1}{3}$ per cent, they would receive a cash benefit of £1.67; at 50 per cent, £2.50; at 100 per cent, £5. The same family earning £14.50, would receive, respectively, £0.16$\frac{1}{2}$; £0.25; and £0.50.

The essential features, then, of such a scheme are: an automatic income and needs test; a tax-paying threshold or some other upper limit above which no benefit is payable; a rate of negative taxation; and a minimum guaranteed income.

I shall confine most of the discussion to NIT for low income families where the father is in work. It is mainly poverty in this group, whom the Supplementary Benefits Commission cannot help, that most NIT plans put forward in Britain are apparently designed to eliminate.

The development of NIT

It is generally acknowledged that the scheme, in its pure form, originated in the United States, in the fertile brain of Professor Milton Friedman. In his book *Capitalism and Freedom*,[81] described on the cover as 'a leading economist's view of the proper role of competitive capitalism', we learn that this 'proper role' has been progressively eroded by growing state intervention in such diverse fields as tariffs, rent control, minimum wage rates, social security programmes, public housing, national parks and, beyond a very basic minimum level, education.

His main argument against such State encroachment is that it diminishes the freedom of the individual. In restoring this freedom and restoring competitive capitalism to its proper role, Friedman is faced with several interconnected problems. One is the existence of this massive and dangerous public sector; a second is the tiresome perpetuation of sizeable pockets of poverty whose condition is to some extent alleviated, however inefficiently, precisely by the 'indiscriminate' public policy measures which he would dismantle; finally, there is the problem of enabling the poor to pay market prices for commodities they now receive 'free', without at the same time 'distorting the market or impeding its functioning'. 'One recourse, and in many ways the most desirable, is private charity',[82] he tells us. If, as is likely, this proves inadequate, some form of state action becomes inevitable : 'the arrangement that recommends itself on purely mechanical grounds is a negative income tax'.[83] To Friedman, the attractions of such a plan are obvious : only the poor are helped; and the estimated cost is substantially lower than existing expenditure on welfare payments and programmes; interference with the market is minimal; in fact, the poor are likely to become more rational economic men. Moreover, all this is achieved without introducing radical redistributive measures. Egalitarianism has known more passionate advocates than Professor Friedman.

Similar proposals have followed in the U.S.;[84] and although

President Nixon's new Family Assistance Program is welcomed, by Sir John Walley, as a family allowance scheme, it is, in fact, a form of NIT.[85]

In Britain, the Labour Party, in its 1964 election manifesto, proposed the use of tax returns to circumvent some of the problems of means-tested National Assistance for the old and for widows. This 'Income Guarantee'[86] is one variant of NIT. Under it, the amount by which income fell short of 'needs', as shown in the tax return, was to be made up at the rate of £1 per £ (in others words, the negative tax rate would have been 100 per cent). For various practical reasons, the plan was abandoned when Labour came to power and the supplementary benefit scheme of 1966 was the result of subsequent re-thinking.

It was never envisaged that the working man and his family could, or should, be included. Perhaps surprisingly, the first attempt so to extend the idea was made by CPAG in 1965,[87] though as this was put forward as one of two alternatives, the Group's commitment to it was perhaps, even then, not a firm one. Tony Lynes has recounted the story of how the idea was dropped in favour of family allowances with clawback.[88] Soon after the Government had committed itself, in 1967, to an increase in family allowances, two NIT proposals were published, by Professor Dennis Lees[89] and Mr Barney Hayhoe.[90] More recently, a multi-disciplinary study group has reviewed the problem and possible alternative policies,[91] and has come down strongly in favour of NIT, which it calls RIT (Reverse income tax). Although the Editor insists that 'The Institute [of Economic Affairs] and its Advisory Council do not necessarily subscribe to the analysis and content of the Report',[92] this will hereafter be referred to as the IEA study. An important distinction needs to be drawn between the IEA and the Lees and Hayhoe schemes. In the former, NIT is viewed as an all-purpose measure, designed to solve the problem of poverty as a whole; in other words, it would be a replacement for most current social security benefits. On the other hand, Lees and Hayhoe would restrict its coverage, initially at least, to families where the father is working.

The social dividend: an alternative strategy

It has recently been argued[93] that there is no difference of substance between NIT and another idea which has a somewhat longer history.[94] This is the social dividend (SD). Briefly, SD guarantees a minimum income by means of a universal cash payment to all households, the size of payment depending on various factors like number and age of children, whether or not the father is working, etc. *All* private income is then taxed. Such schemes *can* be constructed in such a way that they are identical in their effects (same final income at all initial income levels, same marginal rate of tax, same effective rate of tax) to some NIT schemes. However, NIT entails the abolition of universal allowances, SD their extension; NIT is usually designed to reduce Government expenditure (see below), SD inevitably increases it. Perhaps most important, SD is proposed in the context of general taxation reform and carries with it implications for general taxation policy, which is not so with NIT. By contrast, in arguing for a specific rate of negative tax *below* the tax threshold, exponents of NIT are not in any way committing themselves to what should happen *above* it. And yet the argument by which Brown and Dawson[95] contrive to demonstrate that SD and NIT are indistinguishable presupposes precisely this.

The differences, then, between the schemes are arguably greater than the similarities, a point which the authors of the IEA study have been quick to emphasise. I propose to say little more about SD. In the context in which the current proposals in the political arena are being made and from the glimpses one occasionally gets of the plans envisaged, it is clear that what is being debated is nearer to NIT than to SD. It is to the political arena that I now wish to turn.

The political debate

One way of helping [children in families with resources below the supplementary benefit level] is an increase in family allowances. The long term answer, if there be one, is probably a form of negative income tax, or a device of that nature.

This support for NIT was expressed in the Budget debate 1970 by the late Mr Iain Macleod, then Shadow Chancellor, who went on to emphasise that any doubts he felt related to the scheme's detailed administration, in particular to the problem of identification, rather than to any major issues of principle.[96] Even if he had been the only devotee of NIT to be found in the Conservative Party, Mr Macleod's support for it would have commanded attention. He was not. As early as November 1967, Lord Balniel, then Conservative spokesman on Social Security, declared his support. At first, he was rather tentative : 'Just as there are tax tables under the PAYE scheme for the taxes which have to be paid, so it is surely feasible to devise family benefit tables so that family benefit will be paid out weekly, taking into account the earnings and the responsibilities of the families concerned'.[97] Only four months later, however, he was to write a highly laudatory foreword to Hayhoe's pamphlet which claimed to do just that.

An enthusiastic and eloquent endorsement of Professor Lees's NIT scheme has been given by a Vice-Chairman of the Conservatives' Health and Social Security Committee, Mr Tim Fortescue,[98] while Miss Rosemary Marten, of the Conservative Research Department, has stated that opponents of NIT tend to 'throw it out on grounds of impracticability rather than ideology',[99] and she proceeds, on this assumption of shared values, to discuss the technical difficulties, which she finds formidable. Certainly she does not appear to share Mr Macleod's view that identification is the major, if not the only, difficulty.

This impression of Conservative solidarity on NIT has not been achieved by selective quotation. In fact, I have been unable to find any Conservative who has argued against the scheme, and the party's 1970 election manifesto, without making a firm commitment, expressed support for the idea. Most Conservatives seem not to share Miss Marten's relative pessimism about the practical difficulties and the manifesto accused the Labour Government of exaggerating these.[100]

Practical difficulties figured prominently in the Labour Government's rejection of NIT as a way of providing social security for the aged and, implicitly, for others with low incomes.[101] While there is evidence to suggest that the Labour party is less enthusiastic about NIT,[102] there does appear to be a minority of supporters, the most forthright of whom have been Mr Douglas Houghton and Mr Michael Barnes. Mr Houghton, the former Social Services overlord has written : 'Not only could the structure of PAYE and its ingenious and flexible coding system and tax tables be used to provide an automatic minimum income, it could be adapted to a scheme for payment for state services'.[103] Mr Barnes's position is not transparently clear. He accepts Professor Titmuss's general arguments in favour of a universalist infrastructure, on top of which, he feels, 'there is room for selectivity . . . if an accepted way of introducing it can be found. Such a way is the negative income tax solution . . .'[104] This could be interpreted as support *both* for family allowances *and* for NIT. He goes on to say that 'such a system used properly could be a genuine Socialist instrument to redistribute wealth'. The assumptions of 'proper' use and of a universalist infrastructure are important caveats; it seems reasonable to conclude that, whatever their formal similarities, Mr Barnes's rather embryonic scheme differs radically from the Conservative one(s) in its practical impact, its long-term objectives and its theoretical justification.

To judge the attitudes of other Ministers in the Labour Government, one is forced to construct these, in some cases, from more general arguments about selectivity and, in others, from their support for alternative measures which are not compatible with NIT. In the 1967 debate in which Lord Balniel, Mr Fortescue and Mr Barnes declared their positions, Mrs Judith Hart, then Minister of Social Security, advanced seven arguments which had convinced her that family allowances should not be means-tested.[105] Three of these would probably no longer hold under a NIT, as opposed to a 'traditional' means-tested, scheme; the force of the other four, however, remains undiminished, and these are essentially matters of principle : NIT would be a direct, explicit subsidy to low wages; it would involve a tacit acceptance of the evils and inequalities which produce 'haves' and 'have-nots'; it would have harmful effects on incentives; and it would provide no help for those just above the line.

The position adopted by the former Secretary of State for Social Services, Mr Richard Crossman, is perhaps best judged in the light of his Herbert Morrison memorial lecture.[106] Here he distinguished between poverty among those groups who are, in general, outside the labour market, the old, sick, disabled, widowed and unemployed, and those whose problem is inadequate wages. He then explains why, for the old and widowed, it proved impossible to implement the Income Guarantee discussed above, and the reasons he adduces for its abandonment were purely practical ones. In 1964, then, Mr Crossman was not, in principle, averse to NIT for those outside the labour market, nor did he subsequently abandon the idea on grounds of principle. Turning to those working for low wages, he stoutly defends clawback as an effective form of selectivity, which he contrasts starkly with another : means-tested family allowances. He says nothing about NIT : to the extent to which it overcomes *some* of the objections to means-tested family allowances, he might be prepared to moderate his hostility; but if, not unreasonably, we assume that Mr Crossman accepts Mrs Hart's seven-point case against them, then it is difficult to see him as a keen NIT man. Furthermore, his enthusiasm for clawback, 'one of the most ingenious pieces of legislation passed under this Government', is worth comparing with Mr Macleod's support for this measure only as a pre-NIT stop-gap.[107] It should be remembered that family allowances with clawback and NIT are *alternative*, rather than complementary, policies.

It appears that the Liberal position shifted decisively towards NIT during 1969 and 1970. In 1967, the party's spokesman on social security, Mr John Pardoe, argued in favour *both* of higher family allowances financed by reducing tax allowances *and*, later in the same speech, of a negative income tax.[108] At this stage, his fellow-Liberals, Mr Richard Wainwright and Mr Kenneth Guest, both favoured the family allowance solution with clawback.[109] But by some time in 1969, according to Mr Pardoe, the Liberals had been sufficiently deterred by the 'massive disadvantages' of family allowances (in elaborating on this he mentions only the political consequences of their widespread unpopularity) to have 'decided . . . to go for the concept of the negative income tax'.[110]

This account of the political controversy has been presented for two main reasons : to show that NIT is not merely a dream of University economists, but a real political issue which politicians are increasingly talking about and on which they are starting to take sides; and to give a flavour of the quality of the debate and to indicate some of the confusion existing in Westminster over what could become a major dilemma in social policy. The overall impression is that NIT is an issue on which it is now becoming obligatory to have a point of view and that positions are being taken up which are either based on values, assumptions and objectives that remain unstated during the debate or which are arrived at without any searching examination of the larger implications and the likely repercussions.

Unlike Professor Friedman, British exponents of NIT have, perhaps mercifully, not each written a book expounding his or her social philosophy, and the role of social policy and, more specifically, of NIT therein. In Britain, NIT is still looking for its Eleanor Rathbone. One cannot help feeling, however, that this lack of analysis has something to do with the historical situation and the political climate in which the schemes have been developed. As Chapter 1 suggests, family poverty was 'rediscovered' in 1965. The initial reaction, until the Ministry of Social Security confirmed the 'find', was largely one of profound disbelief. The second stage, not surprisingly, was a small flood of panaceas, some of whose details and implications were not, predictably, fully worked out. The quality of the debate so far indicates that not all the politicians have analysed NIT's overall effects, and those that have, have not spelled them out explicitly. It is largely because of this lack of analysis and the resultant confusion that Miss Marten has been able to observe that ideology has played little or no part in the debate.

This conclusion – and it contains a grain of truth – seems to me profoundly dangerous. Few proposals in social policy, particularly those bearing directly on the economy, command the unanimous assent of right, left and centre; and, on an issue like this, when we are told that we all agree on what we are trying to do, it probably means that someone, somewhere, is missing the point.

The case for NIT

We have encountered, among NIT's proponents, a remarkable variation of expectations and intentions. This ranges from the liberated *laissez-faire* paradise of Professor Friedman, at one extreme, to Mr Michael Barnes's socialist millennium at the other. However, most of the arguments in favour of NIT tend to view the goal, or at least the overt goal, as something less ambitious.

I present overleaf, in list form, the arguments, some of them implied, which the advocates of NIT have used to support their case. To avoid a mass of footnotes, I use the following key:

IEA – Institute of Economic Affairs; H – Hayhoe; B – Lord Balniel's introduction to Hayhoe; L – Lees; M – Marten. Numbers are page numbers.

A. NIT provides an automatic device for income supplementation with no risk of non-uptake; it is administratively simple : IEA.33; B.5; H.10; L.9.
B. Its income-needs test is objective and non-discretionary : IEA.34; L.10; B.5; H.10.
C. It is not humiliating : IEA.34; B.5; L.9-10.
D. It concentrates the greatest help where it is most needed; and in doing so is an effective and non-wasteful means of solving the problem of family poverty : IEA.35-36; B.5-6; H.10,16; L.7-9.
E. There is no risk of increased unemployment : IEA.35; H.25.
F. It limits the danger of an inflationary spiral caused by skilled workers' attempting to restore differentials : L.9.
G. It opens up the possibility of major reductions in public expenditure : IEA.36,60-66; B.7.
H. Need is defined in terms of cash, not of category : IEA.36.
I. (Which deserves to be quoted in full): 'Not least RIT [=NIT] would help to replace a multi-structure of well-intentioned pressure groups for particular categories – old age pensioners' associations, the Disablement Income Group, the Child Poverty Action Group, Shelter, Mothers in Action, and numerous more which cause social policy to comprise spasmodic, unco-ordinated and often capricious concessions to persuasive pleading – by a single unambiguous criterion for social assistance . . .'IEA.36-37.
I propose to say nothing more about this, except that students of literary criticism will perhaps find the style intriguing – it is a good example of the bold, forthright, swashbuckling mode of communication beloved of some IEA authors; students of logic might wonder how pressure groups (even in multi-structure) can be replaced by a criterion; and students of social administration could ponder on the mechanism by which NIT is expected to solve the housing problem.
J. Incentive both to work and to increase earnings is retained : H.10-11; 13-15; L.10-11.

K. The wage-stop is effectively abolished : IEA.35; H.13.
L. The existing jungle of means-tested welfare benefits can be abolished : M.9.
M. It helps the one-child family : H.18.
N. Family allowances have, historically, failed to solve the problem of family poverty; NIT will avoid the danger of repeating this failure : L.5,8-9.

Presented in this way, it appears to be a strong case. However, when we examine the arguments more closely we find that several sub-arguments have been knitted together to form an impressive whole; the essential issues are much simpler and more basic than it would appear from this list.

Thus, points A, B and C all belong to the dispute over means-tested benefits and, insofar as NIT may have rivals of the traditional means-test type, the points are valid; but if the debate is over NIT and universal allowances, whatever their detailed features, the issues they raise are irrelevant (if anything, NIT comes off rather worse).

E and F belong mainly to the discussion about minimum wage legislation. The argument is that NIT is an alternative method of tackling the problem of low wages, and is preferable because it would not increase unemployment or cause inflation. John Hughes deals, in Chapter 8, with the substantive points, but, for our purpose, it should be noted that neither E nor F is a criterion for deciding between NIT and universal allowances (except that on point F the latter are slightly preferable : there is less convergence between the take-home pay of low and high wage-earners under a universal allowance scheme than under most NIT schemes).

H does not seem to me to be important *in itself*; it may become significant when we examine the relative effects of different schemes on the people or categories concerned.

J is discussed more fully below; suffice it to say, for the moment, that incentives, far from being an advantage, are a problem created by NIT itself, and do not arise to the same marked and systematic extent with universal allowances.

K, L and M are all true but are not virtues of which NIT possesses a monopoly. K and L also hold under a universal allowance scheme; while CPAG and Sir John Walley both recommend the extension of allowances to the first child. In fact, supporters of NIT should be cautious about pressing L too hard for they are in something of a cleft-stick. Either they superimpose NIT on top of the existing benefits with imponderable effects on marginal tax rates;[111] or they start to abolish these benefits, in which case they may well reduce the real incomes of some of the families they are anxious to help (the ones who have successfully negotiated the labyrinth described in Chapters 2 and 3). Miss Marten[112] is alive to this problem but no one would envy her the task of effecting their phased replacement. Again, there are grounds for preferring the universal allowance solution since it would perform the same function without producing such pronounced side-effects either on marginal tax rates or on poor families.

I have argued that the points considered above, whether taken separately or combined, do not constitute good grounds for preferring NIT to universal allowances; indeed, if anything the reverse is true. The substantive arguments therefore seem to be N and D (together with G which is closely linked to D). The former (that family allowances, viewed historically, have failed to solve the problem of family poverty) is developed by Professor Lees who suggests that this is explained partly by demographic factors, but mainly by inflation. As an historical narrative account of the relations between family allowances, child tax allowances, incomes, and inflationary and demographic trends, this is illuminating, but as an *explanation* for the observed failure of family allowances, it contains some deficiencies. It does not explain why other social security benefits (e.g. retirement pensions), which were more affected by demographic changes, managed to hold their own, and more, against inflation. To argue that family allowances provide only a small part of a household's income whereas retirement pensions constitute the bulk of it (and therefore there are more powerful pressures to guard pensions against inflation) is to beg the question : any conceivable replacement for family allowances would also have provided only a small part of a family's income. Still less does this approach provide a prescription for action. It offers little or no guidance on the crucial issues : whether an alternative would have succeeded between 1946 and the late 1960s; or whether NIT would in future be more inflation-proof than family allowances. Professor Lees adduces no evidence to support this optimistic view about NIT and there seem to be no strong reasons for accepting it. This scepticism may not be justified in the case of the IEA study's scheme. In this, the wage supplement is an integral part of the social security network (which would operate on NIT principles). If, as it is reasonable to assume, there are strong pressures to maintain or increase the real incomes of pensioners, this will operate to the advantage of the low-paid worker and his family.

To argue, then, that family allowances have failed is not, logically, to express a preference for their replacement, as opposed to their improvement. Unless history can be shown to provide us with clearer evidence on the major issues, it would be rash to make a major policy decision on these grounds.

The second argument developed in all the schemes we have examined, is that NIT concentrates help where it is most needed. Although it may not be apparent from the way in which it is usually framed, this argument contains two quite distinct propositions. The first, put simply, is that NIT gives more help to more people who are below a given poverty line than do the alternatives. This is an empirical statement which can be checked by reference to the facts, as has already been done by A. B. Atkinson.[113] I present, below, estimates based on a slightly different hypothesis from that used by Atkinson. The second proposition is that help given to those below the line is necessary, whereas for those above, it is 'unnecessary' or 'wasteful'. This is not empirically verifiable since 'unnecessary' and 'wasteful' contain value judgments and carry with them implications about ends and objectives. Indeed, it may be that the values and objectives will start to become clear when it is made plain exactly what it is that is felt to be 'unnecessary' or 'wasteful'. It is at this point that G comes in : public expenditure and therefore taxation will perhaps be reduced if unnecessary prospective expenditure is not incurred and present wasteful expenditure is cut back.

The case against NIT

(a) *Administrative problems:* We have seen that there is some disagreement, among the advocates of NIT, with regard to the practical difficulties of introducing and operating the scheme. However, they would do well to examine in some detail the questions on the administrative feasibility of NIT posed in the Pensions White Paper and by Professor Richard Titmuss.[114] (Readers who pay meticulous attention to footnotes should be warned that Professor Titmuss did not, in spite of the IEA group,[115] write another book called *Commitment to Compassion*. This is, perhaps, a printer's error or a mis-reading of the title; or it could provide an insight, presumably unintended, into IEA table-talk.) The IEA and Hayhoe do discuss some of these practical problems, though it is debatable whether they resolve them satisfactorily. Lees ignores them completely.

(*b*) *Relative effects on low income households:* One of the main claims for NIT, made by its supporters, is that it gives most help to those in greatest need; this therefore is a question which requires some detailed analysis. When the £0.35 increase in family allowances was announced in mid-1967, it was estimated that approximately half the children then living in families with resources below supplementary benefit (SB) level would be lifted above it.[116] Where comparisons have been made, they have usually been between the effects of this increase and those of a hypothetical NIT scheme implemented at the same time.

Hayhoe is confident about the superiority of his scheme which 'would for all practical purposes eradicate child poverty – it would lift the vast majority of the 160,000 families with half a million children above the poverty line'.[117] Lees does not commit himself so strongly. However, as his 'predilection' is for policy measures designed to ensure a minimum standard of living and since NIT is, he concludes, 'a highly efficient tool of policy',[118] it would be surprising if it did not measure up to his predilections better than do family allowances. The IEA study offers four possible varieties of NIT, and says, of the one which is finally favoured, that 'it guarantees the poverty line minimum income to all'.[119]

Of these three claims, the IEA's can without hesitation be accepted, provided that some mechanism is found by which to include, in the assessment, *real,* as opposed to *average,* housing expenditure. The study group is alive to this problem, which is discussed but not resolved'.[120] On this criterion, therefore, the scheme is more generous than the 1968 increases, though, as we shall see, it can be criticised on other grounds.

The claim made by the IEA study is fairly easy to check because (a) the upper limit at which the proposed allowance is payable is the SB scale; (b) the entire gap between actual income and this limit is filled; and (c) an allowance is specifically made for housing cost. The schemes of Lees and Hayhoe have none of these advantages: the upper limit for the allowance is the tax exemption limit for the family of a given size; one third (Hayhoe) and just under two-fifths (Lees) of the deficit is made up; no allowance for housing is built into the calculation (this means that the relationship between the tax exemption limit and SB level 'needs', which include housing, is a fluctuating one); furthermore, Lees abolishes existing family allowances.

Atkinson presents two estimates of the proportion of families lifted above the then National Assistance level, one calculated from *Circumstances of Families*, the other from the Inland Revenue survey of personal incomes for 1966-7.[121]

Table 1: Effects of Different Schemes on Families with Resources below National Assistance Scale 1966

Percentage raised above N.A. Level by:							
Lees		£0.50 F.A. Increase		CPAG Proposal		Walley Proposal	
I.R.	C.F.	I.R.	C.F.	I.R.	C.F.	I.R.	C.F.
90%	No Estimate 12%	56%	33%	76%	48%	86%	

I.R. – Based on Inland Revenue; C.F. – Based on *Circumstances of Families*.
CPAG proposal in supplement to *Poverty*, No. 2, Spring 1967.
Walley proposal in *The Times*, 11 December 1967.
Source: Atkinson, *op. cit.*, Table 8.5, p. 137; Table 9.2, p. 166.

It is important to recognise that Atkinson presents these as alternative estimates, not as 'better' or 'worse'; in fact, rather different 'populations' are under review. To the extent that *Circumstances of Families* provides a slightly more accurate profile of the incomes of low-paid workers and the amount by

E

which these fall short of their SB level needs, there may be some grounds for preferring an estimate based on this source. Unfortunately, for reasons he gives on p. 164, Atkinson does not attempt to evaluate Lees's proposals by means of this data. Below, I attempt to do this both for Lees and for Hayhoe (whose proposals Atkinson does not discuss). There is one crucial difference in our methods. Atkinson computes average housing expenditure (£2 in 1967), from the Family Expenditure Survey, and applies this to all households. *Circumstances of Families* (Table A17, p. 160) suggests that, for families where resources fall short of needs, this may be a substantial underestimate; and, in any case, it masks a very wide range of housing expenditure. I have therefore adopted three levels of housing expenditure derived from Table A17 to take some account of this variation.

Table 2: Effects of Different Schemes on Families with Resources below Supplementary Benefit Scale 1967

Percentage of Families and Children raised above SB Level by :									
F.A. Increases		Hayhoe		Lees		IEA			
£0.35	£0.50								
(April 1968)	(Oct. 1968)								
Fam.	Chdn.	Fam.	Chdn.	Fam.	Chdn.	Fam.	Chdn.	Fam.	Chdn.
35%	41%	49%	55%	40%	52%	20%	28%	100%	100%

Calculated from *Circumstances of Families*. See the appendix below for assumptions and methods.

NIT schemes which use the tax threshold generally (a) favour the larger family but (b) discriminate against all families with higher housing costs. The reason for (a) is that the tax threshold and supplementary benefit levels diverge as family size increases : in 1968, for a family with three children, all between the ages of 5 and 10, the SB scale was £12 plus rent and the tax threshold, £16.95; for a six child family, the SB level was £16.50 plus rent, the tax threshold £25.45. Higher NIT allowances are therefore payable to the larger families, given the same initial deficit. To turn to (b), a family with rent of £2 and an income deficiency of £1 would receive a substantially higher allowance than the same family with the same deficiency but with a rent of £5; this is because the total income of the second family is nearer the tax threshold. The family allowance solution is slightly more favourable to small families, less so to large ones, and does not contain a systematic bias against high rent payers.

These estimates are highly tentative. If anything, they suggest that not enough is known about the circumstances of low income families to enable us accurately to assess the impact of NIT upon them. But they do indicate that NIT is not the ideal solution that its advocates claim. Compared with recent increases in family allowances its superiority is in some doubt; compared with the proposals of CPAG or Sir John Walley, it is almost certainly less effective. NIT schemes could be made more generous either by raising the tax threshold; increasing the rate of negative tax; or introducing housing expenditure into the assessment (this could be done by a direct housing cost subsidy or by including it as a further tax relief). The difficulty is that these 'solutions' would bring further problems in their wake, either in the form of substantial repercussions throughout the tax structure or of yet higher marginal rates of tax. Furthermore, the scheme would become more expensive.

(c) *Incentives:* Basically, there are two types of incentive which NIT might be expected to affect : the incentive to work; and the incentive (for those who are working) to work harder and earn more. The first, if we view the matter in crudely economic terms and ignore various social and cultural factors, is primarily a question of ensuring that the income of a working man exceeds that which he would get when not at work. If there is a limit below which the latter cannot be depressed, the former must be raised; this, historically, has been one of the strongest arguments for family allowances. NIT could perform the same function. Whether or not it would do so as successfully would depend on the respective levels of negative taxes and family allowances and the relation of both to the level of social security benefits.

The second argument is based on the proposition that high marginal rates of tax discourage the effort needed to earn more; as this rate of tax rises, so leisure becomes correspondingly 'cheaper' and more attractive. This is largely an *a priori* argument which concentrates on what economists call the 'substitution effect'; it ignores the possibility that higher taxes could have the opposite, 'income effect' of encouraging men to work harder in order to maintain their standard of living. No attempt to resolve the theoretical question with empirical evidence on the observed effects of different marginal rates of tax has proved the case either way, as Brown and Dawson conclude after reviewing the evidence.[122] In any case, it would be dangerous to generalise from the effects of taxes on the work-effort of tax-payers to the hypothetical effects of benefits on their recipients.

Since the evidence on *taxes* is so scanty, it comes as no surprise to find that advocates of NIT differ in their estimates of its probable effects on incentives, and therefore disagree about what is an acceptable marginal rate of tax. Hayhoe and Lees favour similar marginal rates ($33\frac{1}{3}$ and $38\frac{3}{4}$ per cent) which, they feel, would not have too marked a disincentive effect. The IEA group, difficult when a reduction in public expenditure is an additional much more boldly, has decided to bridge the whole gap between income and 'need', thus imposing a marginal rate of tax, of £1 per £, on extra earnings below the 'needs' level. Its verdict that 'this is the unavoidable price paid for helping people in need' suggests that the authors are not entirely satisfied with the position into which their logic (of linking benefits for the low wage earner with social security benefits in general) has forced them.

It is worth referring back at this point to the demonstration, above, that the IEA scheme was the most effective in raising families above supplementary benefit level; it now emerges that this was done by imposing a 100 per cent rate of tax on extra earnings. Conversely, Lees and Hayhoe, while endeavouring to preserve incentives, were much less successful in raising families above the line. This illustrates a crucial difficulty in any NIT scheme: generosity and the preservation of incentive are goals which it is scarcely possible to reconcile. It becomes even more goal.

In contrast, family allowances do not have any such generalised disincentive effects though they may make a man liable for tax or increase his rate of tax. But, even at the standard rate, this will still be lower than Hayhoe's proposed rate of negative tax, (32% in 1968, as against $33\frac{1}{3}\%$).[123]

(*d*) *Effects on wages:* Closely associated with the problem of incentives is that of NIT's effects on wage rates. The spectre which NIT raises is that of Speenhamland and its supposed dread consequences: a profligate, improvident, demoralised, pauperised labour force. This of course is much too dramatic. Cuts in wages are improbable. However, NIT can, not unreasonably, be seen as a direct subsidy to low wages. An employer is likely to see little point in paying, and workers and their Unions will have little incentive to press for, a wage increase of £1 if, as under the IEA scheme, £1 is to be deducted from their negative tax payment. This is the extreme case; the Hayhoe and Lees schemes, which allow £0.67 and £0.61, respectively, of each extra £ to be retained, would have less marked effects.

The dilemma which we encountered with regard to incentives recurs here. *Effective* help of the NIT type could have repercussions on wage levels; on the other hand, an attempt to limit these repercussions immediately makes the scheme less effective, or more expensive.

A wider perspective

So far, the case against NIT has been put in terms which implicitly accept the objectives of the scheme's supporters. The time has now come to widen the perspective and introduce other questions which rarely, if ever, receive their attention.

Changes in social policy do not occur in a historical vacuum. New policies are either superimposed on an older structure or they may replace parts of it; similarly, new measures are proposed or introduced within the context of an on-going debate on policy. Some of the arguments and principles accepted and upheld previously may continue to be accepted and upheld; others may be modified or rejected and, in their place, new principles evolve.

The introduction of NIT would entail substantial discontinuities with the past and bring with it major changes of principle, particularly with regard to family allowances. By abolishing family allowances (in the case of the IEA group and Lees) or by freezing them and discounting the possibility of further increases (Hayhoe and Lord Balniel), supporters of NIT are not merely rejecting a strategy for solving the problem of family poverty; they are also denying the attainability or desirability of a range of other objectives which family allowances were designed to achieve. More specifically, one assumes they find unconvincing the classic case for family allowances made by Eleanor Rathbone in 1924.[124] Yet her arguments (or rather one of them) receive less than a page of discussion in the three texts under consideration; at the end of this Lees concludes 'the logic of this argument can, of course, be questioned'.[125] Questionable it may be; questioned it never is, much less refuted. Sir John Walley develops some of Rathbone's ideas in Chapter 9. Here there is time to enlarge upon one of these themes only: that of income redistribution.

NIT and income redistribution

'Inevitably with the family benefit [NIT] scheme poorer families will get more and some better-off families less'.[126] Thus has Hayhoe recognised that NIT can have significant effects on income distribution and not only at and below the poverty line.

Of the three NIT schemes under review, one (Hayhoe's) is so designed that no family can be worse off than it was with family allowances at their 1967 level; the other two (IEA and Lees) replace existing family allowances by NIT. It follows from this that, under these two proposals, families with incomes above a certain level will become worse off under NIT, since the loss of family allowances will not be compensated for by NIT benefits. Similarly, there will be a point under all three schemes at which families will receive less under NIT than the April 1968 increase of £0.35 per child in family allowances gave them.

This is a complex issue and is best approached by setting out, in tabular form, the 'break-even' earnings under NIT, i.e. those below which families are better off with NIT than with family allowances and above which they are worse off (Table 3). Column 1 shows the level at which NIT benefits would cease to be payable (the tax threshold). Column 2 shows the break-even points for NIT compared with family allowances at their 1967 levels. Column 3 compares NIT and family allowances at their April 1968 levels. For comparison, the SB scale then in force is shown in Column 4.

NIT does, of course, redistribute income vertically from the better-off to the worse-off. However, the manner in which it does this is highly discriminatory. Both Lees and the IEA group concentrate help on those in the greatest need largely by means

Table 3: NIT Compared with Family Allowances – 'Break-Even' Earnings in 1968

No. of children (All assumed to be under 11)	Weekly Earnings Above Which Families Would Receive: (1) No NIT Benefit		(2) Less from NIT than from FAs at £0.40 and £0.50			(3) Less from NIT than from FAs at £0.75 & £0.85			(4) SB Scales from Nov. 1967, incl. £3 rent
	Lees & Hayhoe	IEA	Lees	Hayhoe	IEA	Lees	Hayhoe	IEA	
	£	£	£		£	£	£	£	£
1	11.25	11.42½	–		–	–	–	–	11.42½
2	14.10	12.30	13.10	NO	12.40	12.20	12.65	12.05	12.80
3	16.95	14.17½	14.65	ONE	13.27½	12.85	13.95	12.57½	14.17½
4	19.75	15.55	16.15	WORSE	14.15	13.45	15.20	13.10	15.55
5	22.60	16.92½	17.70	OFF	15.02½	14.10	16.50	13.62½	16.92½
6	25.45	18.30	19.25		15.90	14.75	17.80	14.15	18.30

Notes:
(a) The break-even earnings under the IEA scheme were computed on the basis of a £3 weekly housing cost.
(b) Since Lees's and Hayhoe's schemes were introduced largely as a response to the announcement of a £0.35 increase in family allowances, I have compared them with allowances at this level (£0.75 & £0.85); since October 1968 the level has been £0.90 and £1.
(c) As one-child families receive no family allowance, they cannot be worse off under any of the schemes. Hayhoe retains family allowances at their old (£0.40 & £0.50) level, so that under his scheme, unlike Lees's or the IEA's, no family can be worse off than they were with allowances at that level.
(d) SB scale is computed on the assumption that each child attracts an allowance of £1.37½, the mean of the scale rates for under 5s and 5-10 year olds.
(e) Earnings are gross before the deduction of National Insurance, graduated contributions and income tax.

of removing family allowances from those who do not 'need' them. It can be seen, from Table 3, that the earnings level at which Lees estimates a two-child family needs no help at all is £14.10; that at which it needs less help than it was receiving from its old (£0.40) family allowance is £13.10; and that at which it does not need the entire April 1968 family allowance (£0.75) is £12.20. The IEA's concept of need is not very different. Criticising clawback, they say 'since it relies on the structure of income tax to recover unintended benefits, it still distributes benefits indiscriminately to families who are exempt from tax which includes many who are *not* poor'.[127] Just who these 'non-poor' families are can be judged from Table 3. They are those whose earnings lie between the two levels shown in Column 1, except, that, to take account of the 1968 reduction in tax allowances, approximately £0.75 per child for the second and subsequent children should be deducted from the larger figure. Thus, in the eyes of the IEA, 'indiscriminate benefits' were handed out to three-child families where earnings lay in the range of £14.17½ to £15.45.

Hayhoe is rather less punitive: he makes no one worse off (except that NIT has to be paid for). However, Columns 1 and 3 show that he too is rigorously selective in determining who should become better off. To keep these figures in perspective, it should be remembered that in April 1968 average earnings of adult male manual workers in manufacturing industries were £22.82½.

So much for those who are to be helped. Under the IEA and Lees's schemes others are to be penalised since every family loses its family allowance. This measure is not quite as unselective and undiscriminating as it might at first sight appear. Family allowances are taxable, and therefore the impact of their disappearance increases, in *cash* terms, as tax liability and incomes fall. This impact is even more marked when the *relative* effect (the proportion of income lost) is considered. This is a curious measure to come from Lees, who has declared that 'in the past ten years, it would seem that a combination of inflation, higher [tax] allowances and high tax rates have put families paying income tax in a more favoured position. Those relying on family allowances alone to supplement the cost of children have been losing ground.'[128]

The implications of NIT for horizontal redistribution (equity between those in the same income bracket but with different responsibilities) must also be briefly considered. By abandoning family allowances, the supporters of NIT show that they intend to rely exclusively on the income tax structure to perform this role. In Chapter 9, Sir John Walley demonstrates how, within the U.K.'s progressive tax system, this favours the better-off, even when there are family allowances which help redress the balance in favour of those with reduced or zero tax commitments. With their disappearance, the balance would shift sharply in favour of those with higher tax liabilities.

To sum up, the supporters of NIT, by virtue both of what they recommend and what they abandon and reject, would substantially reduce the redistributive role of the state, by confining the receipt of benefits to the very poor, and doing so largely at the expense of the slightly less poor, who under some schemes would lose their existing family allowances and under all the schemes are judged to need no extra or alternative state help. Far from being accidental, this result is rooted in the view of poverty held by NIT's adherents, to which we now turn.

View of poverty implied by NIT

There are two main models or views of poverty. The first, which has a history stretching back to the social surveys of the late nineteenth century, sees poverty as a line: above it are the non-poor; below it, the poor. The aim of anti-poverty programmes is to ensure that everyone is lifted above the line. On this view, what happens above the line has nothing to do with the problem of poverty; instead, the quite different question of inequality is introduced. This, of course, may or may not be seen as a 'problem'.

The second view starts from the premiss that poverty and inequality are conceptually inseparable: the total social structure is permeated by massive and systematic inequalities of income and wealth which interlock with, reinforce and are reinforced by inequalities of educational opportunity and provision, health standards and care, housing conditions and employment conditions and prospects. Poverty is the extreme manifestation of this structural inequality.

These opposing models do not merely reflect different theoretical perspectives; they also profoundly affect social strategy. On the first view, the State should confine itself to income supplementation, designed to lift the poor (usually seen as a declining remnant category) above the poverty line; income redistribution is thus restricted to those policies which impinge directly upon the poor, while programmes which have spill-over effects above the line are seen as 'unnecessary'. By contrast, supporters of the second view argue that their opponents totally misconceive the nature and size of the problem and therefore underestimate the scale of the measures needed to combat it. What is needed is a much broader and more determined assault on all the areas of inequality, in which priority is given to the removal of the worse inequalities.

The logic of NIT places its supporters very clearly in the first camp. But here they are faced with a dilemma. A universalist solution along the lines proposed by Sir John Walley or CPAG would, as far as can be judged, be *more* effective than NIT in achieving the limited objectives pursued by NIT's advocates; they are therefore logically forced to accept some such proposal or to improve NIT. On the other hand, the view of poverty implied by NIT and its overall effects on income distribution, will convince others, who see poverty and inequality not as distinct entities but as structurally related phenomena, that NIT is a strategy to be viewed with considerable suspicion.

Wider implications for social policy

We have seen that for Friedman, the inventor of NIT, much of the attractiveness of the scheme is that it coheres very well with his overall social and economic philosophy. In Britain, its advocates have generally been less explicit about ultimate goals though the Open Group appreciate the danger, as they see it, of being too closely associated with Professor Friedman.[129] It would, of course, be unjustifiable to suggest that, in the absence of similar disclaimers, other advocates of NIT want it to perform broadly the same role as does Friedman, namely to enable the poor to pay market prices and so to facilitate the withdrawal of the State from areas they regard as the legitimate preserve of private enterprise.

However, the evidence that some of them may see it in a

similar light is not entirely lacking. Professor Lees[130] has argued that medical care is, and should be treated as, just another economic 'good'. Arthur Seldon,[131] one of the IEA study group, has argued for the progressive disengagement of the state from the fields of pensions and health. It would perhaps be neither fanciful nor unjust, therefore, to suggest that these authors see NIT as an important part of this strategy, namely a mechanism by which to overcome one flaw of the market solution, the inability of some people to pay market prices. In fact, the case for the private market is developed in the IEA study. The authors discuss three major possibilities following the introduction of NIT: tax remission and self-provision in health for the higher income groups; a scheme by which those below middle age could opt out of the State pension system; and the return of housing to the open market (with a direct cash subsidy to low-income families to enable them to compete).[132]

Lord Balniel has sketched in relatively few details of his vision of the future after NIT's installation. However, from his introduction to Hayhoe's pamphlet it emerges that his objectives may be not so very different from those pursued by the IEA. The relevant passage is worth quoting in full:

> It [Hayhoe's scheme] is based on a concept which might gradually be widened to become a coherent social strategy to help the poorest and most unfortunate. Instead of an ever-increasing weight of taxation to provide universal benefits to deal with the diminishing sector of the community living in poverty, it makes possible a reduction in the general level of taxation. In doing so it encourages those who are able to stand on their own feet, to be independent, to be increasingly self-reliant and to exercise their own personal freedom of choice.[133]

The introduction of these wider policy issues at this stage, as part of the case *against* NIT, involves a value judgment on my part. They could equally well have been cited as part of the case *for*, as Professor Lees, the IEA and perhaps Lord Balniel would prefer. The reader, too, may wish to transpose this section. The main point, however, is that if NIT is part of a 'coherent social strategy' of this type it would be as well if the scope of the present debate were enlarged to embrace this extra dimension. The policy now becomes something more than 'concentrating help on those

in the greatest need' and, as with income redistribution and the
view of poverty, ideology starts to loom rather larger than
impracticability.

Conclusion

It has been asserted more than once in IEA, and related, literature[134] that egalitarianism and humanitarianism are incompatible principles, and that those who espouse the former, especially
in the guise of universal social services, necessarily (whether
consciously or not) reject the latter. The true humanitarians, it is
argued, are the selectivists who concentrate help where it is most
needed (and who would usually leave the better-off majority to
fend for themselves). It is, of course, this second role which NIT's
advocates arrogate to themselves.

In assessing the validity of this claim it is best to keep two
issues distinct. First, which policy is most humane, i.e. a more
effective weapon in the war against poverty? Secondly, is egalitarianism, in this area, incompatible with humanitarianism? The
evidence collected in this chapter suggests that NIT is considerably less humane than its advocates claim. Of the schemes so far
put forward, only one solves the problem of poverty, narrowly
defined (and in doing so it sets in train a series of further problems which are unique to this 'solution'); the others, in deliberately avoiding the worst of these side-effects, are correspondingly
less effective and less humane. Furthermore, humanitarianism for
the very poor is bought at the cost of neglecting, even impoverish-
ing the not-quite-so-poor : for it is they who stand to gain from
increased family allowances, which, it is felt, they do not need;
and they who will suffer most from the withdrawal of their
existing allowances, which they can apparently manage without.
Humanitarianism surely demands of its disciples a broader perspective than they have so far taken in evaluating NIT's qualities.
The 1968 family allowance increases have been criticised by
universalists and selectivists alike as inadequate, and by the latter
as misconceived in principle. In fact, it seems that they have been
as effective as two of the rival NIT proposals would have been.
But these increases are not the last ditch defence of universalists
and egalitarians. It is possible, as CPAG and Sir John Walley
have shown, to achieve the stated objectives of the humane

selectivist without adopting his methods, without setting in motion a series of dangerous side-effects and without losing sight of other important goals.

This answers the second question about humanitarianism and egalitarianism. It is possible to have both. Selectivists have argued that slavish devotion to egalitarianism is responsible for the supposed inadequacy and inhumanity of universalist solutions. One wonders whether it is not hostility to egalitarianism which leads NIT's supporters to demand a solution which is in many ways less humane, and unquestionably less egalitarian.

6 The family income supplement

DAVID BARKER

The Conservatives came to power in June 1970 with a clear statement of intent to increase family allowances, with clawback, as 'the only way of tackling family poverty in the short term'.[135] On 28 October 1970, however, the new government published a bill which signified a radical departure not only from its stated policy in opposition but from any previous attempt in this country, at least in the recent past, to grapple with the problem of relating income to family size. In *some* ways it resembles NIT; but again, there are significant differences.

The new measure

The *Family Income Supplements Bill*[136] received its Second Reading on 10 November 1970 and became law on 17 December 1970.

The aim of the Act is to supplement the incomes of families where the breadwinner is in full-time work for a low wage and which the SBC is, at present, unable to help. Its general principles are fairly easily understood. Difficulties are likely to arise, however, over definitions of some of the terms introduced, such as 'remunerative full-time work'; 'normally engaged in'; 'household'; and 'normal gross income'. The Act lays down the gross income or 'prescribed amount' (which includes family allowances currently payable) below which families will qualify for the supplement. The supplement will be half the difference between the prescribed amount and the normal gross income.

There is, however, a maximum to the supplement that any family may receive. This was originally set at £3 per week, with provision for the Secretary of State to amend it by regulations; on 24 March 1971, he announced that the limit would be raised to £4.[137] In the same statement, he raised the prescribed amount from £15 to £18 for a 'family' with one child, regardless of whether it has one parent or two. The Act's provision for £2 to be added to the prescribed amount for each additional child remained unchanged.

The combined effects of these provisions can be seen if we consider a man earning £16 per week gross. With one child, he will qualify for a supplement of £1; if he had three children, he would already be getting £1.90 in family allowance, so his supplement would be £2.10 (rounding up to the nearest £0.10); with seven children, he would (just) be subject to the £4 maximum condition, since the difference between his income (£21.90 with family allowance) and the prescribed amount (£30) exceeds £8.

The decision to adopt an *ad hoc* income limit, bearing no relation to the tax system or tax threshold, has meant that one of the advantages claimed for NIT – automatic 100 per cent uptake[138] – will not obtain. FIS will now be payable only after an individual application has been made to, and investigated by, the SBC. Payment will be made, however, by the Department of Health and Social Security, not by the Commission. Once a claim has been accepted, the supplement will be paid for six months, after which a further application has to be submitted.

This summary covers the main provisions of the Act. Other clauses cover appeals, legal proceedings, changes which may be made by regulations and so on.

Why FIS?

It is noteworthy that a large proportion of the speech of the Secretary of State, Sir Keith Joseph, moving the Bill's Second Reading, was devoted to explanations of why other approaches, especially family allowances with clawback, would be less effective than FIS. Since therefore much of the case for FIS has rested on the weaknesses of the available alternatives, these points deserve close scrutiny. They are:

(a) that the family allowance solution could do nothing for the one child family (and about one-third of the families FIS is designed to help contain only one child).

(b) family allowances could not provide the 'scale of help' required, 'that is, not without going into astronomic figures'.

(c) following the tax changes introduced in the Budgets of 1969 and 1970, the scope of clawback was smaller than was generally realised.[139]

The first point is a valid one and was accepted by the Opposition Spokesman, Mrs Shirley Williams. The stated objection to an additional allowance for the first child is that it could not come into operation until mid-1972.[140] Probably more important would be the projected cost, which Mr Crossman put at £80 million (presumably net after tax and clawback).[141] The *gross* cost of family allowances for the first child set at £1 would exceed £300 million which alone might justify the epithet 'astronomic'. Such an innovation, accompanied by an increase in existing allowances with clawback, would have been difficult to put over with the October 1970 package, whose aim was to cut public expenditure and taxation. It can thus be seen that Treasury policy profoundly influenced the range of options open to the Secretary of State, and the decision to opt for FIS has to be set in the context of the October 1970 measures as a whole.

This problem can best be considered in the light of Sir Keith's other two objections to the family allowance solution. These go closely together. The argument that the scope of clawback is reduced by the 1969 and 1970 changes in the tax threshold is dealt with in Chapter 10; and as Frank Field reports in Chapter 12, CPAG has advocated a lifting of the threshold in order to facilitate a further increase in family allowances with clawback.

It is at this point that the Chancellor's package announced on 27 October 1970 becomes highly relevant. The cuts in public expenditure amounted to an estimated £330 million in 1971-72. 'As a consequence', Mr Barber went on, 'I have decided that the standard rate of income tax will be cut by [$2\frac{1}{2}$p]'.[142] The loss of revenue to the Exchequer was computed at £315 m. in the first year and £350 m. in a full year. We observe that Mr Barber had some £300-350 m. to give back to the tax-payer. As Brian Abel Smith has observed, reducing the standard rate by $2\frac{1}{2}$p was not the only course of action open to him. Two available alternatives, he suggests, were a minimum earned-income allowance or the restoration of reduced rates of tax – 'a much fairer way of cutting income tax'.[143] The effect of either alternative (or both) would immediately have been to raise the level at which the standard rate of tax became payable and so to clear the way perhaps for an allowance for the first child and/or additional family allowances. Whether these were to be taxable or tax-free, clawed back in full, in part or not at all, were all matters which could have been negotiated and finely balanced.

Of course the problem is much more complicated than this. Other Ministers would not take kindly to a manoeuvre whereby, as they saw it, their spending was being cut to allow the Department of Health and Social Security to pay more and bigger family allowances. And it might further be argued, but could not be proved, that a reduction in the standard rate was necessary to increase incentives. But it remains true that any argument which maintains the impracticability or ineffectiveness of further applications of clawback is premissed on the assumption that the tax system cannot be adjusted to allow clawback to operate.

This was not the position in October 1970. The case for a selective reduction in taxation for the lower income groups has also been argued on rather different grounds by Turner and Wilkinson. They have analysed the relationship between wages, taxes and other stoppages over the years 1959-1970 and shown how tax thresholds have been lowered towards the end of the period.[144]

The argument that FIS was the only way out is therefore not entirely convincing. Its validity rests on the acceptance of Mr Jenkins's tax changes, and these were, arguably, somewhat short-sighted, *ad hoc* expedients whose effect was to reduce the overall progressiveness of the tax system.

The advantages of FIS

The main strength of the new Act is that, for the first time, the one child family is brought within the ambit of wage supplementation programmes; it has also been recognised that in low income families with several children, financial burdens are imposed by the eldest child. Sir Keith Joseph has estimated that

F

a third of the families entitled to help under the Act contain one child only.[145] It is far from clear, however, on what data this is based and therefore how reliable his estimate is.[146]

Not only is the one-child family helped, but it is also recognised that any policy to help families with more than one child will be abortive unless an allowance is made for the eldest child. The principle is embodied in this Act as it has never been in family allowance legislation past and present.

The single parent family (where the parent is working) comes out comparatively well from FIS. This can be seen from a comparison between FIS figures and SB rates. Holding family size, age of children and housing expenditure constant, we find that the SB scale rate for a family with one parent is consistently £3.30 lower than for one with two adults, whereas the prescribed amount remains the same. Take two families, one containing husband and wife, the other a widow, each with two children, 6 and 8 years old, and both paying £4 for housing; the father and the widow both earn £14. In each case, the prescribed amount (£20) and gross income before FIS (£14.00 plus £0.90 family allowance) is the same, and both would receive the same FIS benefit: £2.60. Before stoppages, however, one family is £0.10 above its SB level requirements, while the other is £3.70 above.

However, the real benefit which the single parent family will receive from FIS will depend on a multitude of other factors, notably the local provision of day care facilities and the charges made for them. It is further worth noting that most single parent households consist of mother and children rather than father and children; and since women's wages are consistently lower than men's, it may well be that women who might have applied for FIS would be affected by the £4 limit, and would still be better off not working (or working part-time) and claiming supplementary benefit.

Finally, it can be confidently asserted that benefits paid under the FIS scheme will go only to those in the greatest need. What is less certain is whether all those in the greatest need will receive FIS and whether the help they receive will be adequate.

The shortcomings of FIS

The criticisms to which FIS is exposed are largely those which have already been levelled, in the previous chapter, at NIT. However, there are additional points which will be taken first. One of the main weaknesses of FIS is precisely that it forgoes one of the major advantages claimed for NIT (which family allowances share), namely, the automatic nature which guarantees 100 per cent uptake. Uptake of FIS will therefore depend on the interplay of several factors. Will publicity be adequate? Will entitlement to FIS as a *right* be convincingly conveyed? Will it prove possible to overcome the reluctance of many potential recipients to admit their poverty and have their circumstances investigated? How will FIS and its claimants be viewed by the public at large? As Tony Lynes has shown, in Chapter 2, past experience is not encouraging – even when a means-tested benefit is publicised as a right.

His review of FIS's antecedents does not suggest that much confidence can be placed in a means-tested scheme which depends on the self-selection and initiative of those who are entitled. The assumption that some will fall through the net is, indeed, built into the cost estimates contained in the Bill's Financial Memorandum. As Sir Keith Joseph has explained, these have been computed on the basis of an 85 per cent take-up rate.[147] On the other hand, Peter Townsend has suggested that the Act may cost as little as £3 million (compared with the official estimate of £8 million) presumably because of a shortfall of claimants.[148]

The predictions, both of the Act's critics and of its sponsors, are little more than guesswork. Ultimately, the effectiveness of FIS will have to be tested in operation. Here, further difficulties are likely to arise because of the lack of up-to-date information on low incomes.[149]

The scheme's operating costs and its tendency towards bureaucratic complication may also be criticised. The Financial Memorandum predicts that £600,000 annually will be spent on administration and £8 million on benefits. This ratio of administrative cost to benefit provided is far higher than in the family allowance scheme, and would become even higher if there were a shortfall of applicants. Furthermore, the Memorandum's estimate of 200 extra civil servants has been criticised as unrealistically low both by Mr Richard Crossman and by a Conservative specialist in social security, Sir Brandon Rhys-

Williams.[150] For the families concerned, it involves yet another extra means-test, though it is intended to link FIS to NHS exemptions and other welfare benefits. Co-ordination of this sort could prove to be another advantage of FIS.

The above outline of those shortcomings in FIS which do not apply to NIT should not obscure the more fundamental point that the major criticisms of FIS are precisely those which have been already directed at NIT. Basically, these concern the generosity and effectiveness of the scheme, and, associated with this, its effects on incentives and wages, and the implications of FIS for the Government's social strategy.

It has become customary to evaluate anti-poverty measures by their effectiveness in raising those below the poverty line up to or above the line (SB level). Judged by this simple criterion, FIS does not emerge with any great credit. Sir Keith claimed only that it would 'help over half the households below the poverty line'.[151] Help for the other half, he suggested, would come in the form of an extended rent rebate scheme; since this is another strand of the Government's anti-poverty campaign, its probable effects are considered below.

The statement that FIS is intended to help half the households in poverty says nothing about the amount or effectiveness of the help they will receive. Table 4 sets out the relationship between the 'prescribed amount' under FIS and the SB scale.

Table 4: Relationship between the FIS Prescribed Amount and the Supplementary Benefit Scale, 1971

Children in Family	Prescribed Amount £	S.B. Scale from Nov. 1971 £
1	18	11.60
2	20	13.70
3	22	15.80
4	24	17.90
5	26	20.00

Notes:

1. £2.15 is allowed on the SB scale for each child. This is the average benefit for children aged 0-15 years.
2. No allowance is made for rent on the SB scale.

It can be seen, from Table 4, that the SB scale is consistently

£6.00 to £6.40 below the corresponding prescribed amount. This means that if a family's housing costs are approximately at this level, their needs and their FIS ceiling will be the same; where rents are lower, the FIS ceiling will exceed SB scale needs, but for those paying higher rents, SB needs will be greater. Consequently, the FIS benefit will not be sufficient to bring the incomes of the high rent-payer up to the poverty line. Even those with medium and low rents will not necessarily reach the poverty line : *half* the difference between income and prescribed amount is paid in FIS benefit; and the SB scale is computed on the basis of net available resources after stoppages, while the FIS ceiling applies to gross income. £1.50 would be a reasonable sum to deduct for insurance contributions and necessary expenses incurred at work. When an adjustment is made for these two factors it becomes clear that the effectiveness of FIS is considerably reduced. Of course, differences in rent levels, family size and weekly earnings conspire to create a complex situation. However the broad effects of FIS can be assessed from Table 5.

The important comparison to be made on the basis of the figures in Table 5 is between net available resources and needs as assessed on the SB scale. Two major conclusions can be derived from the table : large families are less likely to be brought up to SB level; and the higher the rent, the less likely it is that a family's income will be raised to this level. More large families remain below the poverty line because when earnings are held constant, the combined income for each child from family allowances and FIS is still smaller than the child's needs on the supplementary benefit scale. The effect of this disparity is cumulative. The importance of high rent as a cause of poverty has already been emphasised, and the recognition of this fact has played a significant part in the formulation of the Government's policy.

In the light of Sir Keith Joseph's assertion[152] that half the families in poverty (those not helped by FIS) will be assisted either by rationalised and concentrated housing subsidies in the public sector or by the extension of rent rebates to the private sector, this aspect of the Government's policy requires some examination. Details of the income scales and limits, the minimum rebated rent payable and the way in which the fair rents are to be assessed, have not been announced at the time of

Table 5

Effect of FIS on families with earnings of £14 and £16 per week

Children in family	Prescribed Amount	SB needs, given housing expenditure of:				Earnings of £14		Earnings of £16	
		£2	£3	£4	£5	FIS benefit	net available resources after FIS benefit	FIS benefit	net available resources after FIS benefit
	£	£	£	£	£	£	£	£	£
1	18	13.60	14.60	15.60	16.60	2.00	14.50	1.00	15.50
2	20	15.75	16.75	17.75	18.75	2.60	16.00	1.60	17.00
3	22	17.90	18.90	19.90	20.90	3.10	17.50	2.10	18.50
4	24	20.05	21.05	22.05	23.05	3.60	19.00	2.60	20.00
5	26	22.20	23.20	24.20	25.20	4.00	20.40	3.10	21.50
6	28	24.35	25.35	26.35	27.35	4.00	21.40	3.60	23.00

Notes:

1. See Table 4, note 1.
2. Net available resources are calculated on the basis that stoppages and working expenses total £1.50.
3. For each family size, the appropriate family allowance has been incorporated in the calculation.

writing. However, some observations can be made. First, it can be seen from Table 5 that with housing costs set at £3, all families with earnings of £14, and many with £16, will still be below SB level. To be effective, therefore, rebates in the private sector will need to be large ones in many cases. Secondly, the extended rebate scheme will still not cover furnished tenancies.[153] While still forming a minority of the privately rented sector, furnished accommodation has increased its share since the Rent Act, 1965, which gave security of tenure to 'unfurnished tenants'. The Francis Committee's recommendation, which has now been accepted by the Government,[154] that the security conferred by the 1965 Act should not be extended to 'furnished tenants', may well hasten this trend. Thirdly, what is effectively a pilot scheme for rebates in the private sector has been operating, since 1970, in Birmingham. The early indications are that only a small fraction of those eligible have applied.[155] Otherwise the uptake of rent rebates cannot be calculated; but evaluations of some of the schemes in operation[156] do not inspire confidence. Certainly, rent officers will need to play a more active and interventionist role than the 1965 Rent Act has allowed them.[157] Finally, the Government's projection of public expenditure does not suggest that the scheme will be particularly generous. In his announcement of the October 1970 measures, the Chancellor of the Exchequer stated his intention to save between £100 and £200 millions on housing subsidies by the mid-1970s.[158] This reduced sum will finance the rebates in both the local authority and the private sector, while the previous administration had earmarked the larger sum for the local authority sector. In spite of these reservations, the attempts to rationalise central government subsidies to local authorities and to treat more equitably tenants in both private and public sectors are welcome and overdue. The real question is whether they will work and whether the scale of help will be sufficient.

Another consequence of FIS and of the new rebates will be greatly to increase the marginal rate of tax on the low paid. In the second reading debate, Sir Keith Joseph, defending FIS against criticisms that its benefits were inadequate, argued that a more generous scheme could have serious effects on incentives (that is, if the rate of benefit were higher than the proposed £0.50 in the £). We can observe, in passing, that another way of making FIS more generous without increasing marginal tax rates would be to increase the FIS ceilings (the 'prescribed amount'). The main point is, however, that Sir Keith appears to regard the marginal rate of 50 per cent contained in the Bill as acceptable, which means that he is prepared to tolerate a somewhat higher rate than were Lees or Hayhoe (see Chapter 5). But while £0.50 of FIS is lost for every extra £1 earned at the margin, the family will in addition lose their rate rebate (at about £0.12½ per £), their rent rebate (at a rate as yet unspecified) and will pay an extra 4p to 5p in graduated and earnings-related contributions. Many will still have to pay income tax.[159] The situation reached in this piecemeal, cumulative fashion is almost exactly that which Sir Keith was trying to avoid in deciding the appropriate rate of benefit under FIS. The problem can be briefly stated. A complex of benefits has already grown up, some operated nationally; others locally but on national scales; and others locally and on local scales. Some are tapered evenly; others are arranged in steps, so that at certain critical income levels entitlement to a benefit or to a large part of it is lost completely. Their effects on marginal rates of tax are therefore unpredictable and capricious; but because in general they have affected fairly narrow income bands, the combined effect has been a large one. Two additional schemes are now to be superimposed on these, not as peripheral measures to exempt the poor from charges, but as integral elements of an income supplementation programme. FIS (and probably rent rebates) will also apply over a narrow range of incomes; and below the FIS ceiling the standard rate of tax starts to bite. The introduction of FIS and the new rent rebates will thus impose even higher marginal rates of tax on the lower income groups than those documented in studies of existing welfare benefit schemes.[160]

It has already been shown, in Chapter 5, that the connection between a given marginal rate of tax and work incentive is far from securely established; but what is worth noting here is first that the consequences of the Government's policies for the poor directly contradict both its stated intentions and the actions it has taken to assist the better off, and second that the actual marginal rate of tax on the income of FIS recipients will be substantially higher than the level held by Sir Keith Joseph to be acceptable.

The argument about incentives is of course redolent of the Speenhamland controversy and, not surprisingly, 'Speenhamland' was a word which cropped up more than once in the debate on the second reading. Sir Keith Joseph introduced it simply to dismiss it, arguing that 'the contrast with this Bill is startling': in particular, 'there was no organised trade union movement' in 1795, while today 'the trade union movement is strong'; and while 'Speenhamland came to affect the majority of rural workers', FIS 'will bring help to well under 1 per cent of working households'.[161] Other participants were less convinced, disturbed not so much by the Bill itself as by the principle it embodied and the consequences if it were extended. The debate ranged over the problems of incentives, wage levels, the risk of abuse and the moral and economic dangers of giving relief in supplementation of wages. Indeed some fears may have been strengthened by the Government's own anxieties about incentive effects and abuses.[162] However, the Cassandra-like forebodings of Mr Enoch Powell ('we shall no doubt give the Bill a Second Reading tonight, but many of those who vote for it or let it go through will live to regret what we have done')[163] will perhaps prove unduly pessimistic. He was right, nevertheless, to see the Bill as the beginning of a departure from principles that had thereto been firmly upheld.

In itself, FIS is a small measure, both in the size of public expenditure involved and in the impact it can be expected to have on the problem of poverty; family allowances will remain for most families the major source of wage supplementation and these FIS leaves untouched. It is perhaps best viewed, therefore, as a tentative prelude to later, larger scale measures whose form will be largely determined by the lessons learned from FIS. Indeed, the Secretary of State suggested this when he said 'during the election campaign, this Government pledged itself to tackle family poverty over the lifetime of this Parliament. The Bill now before us is the first step in our policy'.[164] Two concluding thoughts will be offered, one referring to the short term, the other to the long term. First, FIS has been presented by the Government as a necessary expedient whose shape was dictated by the tax structure bequeathed to them by their predecessors. The contention that this made clawback a non-starter is discussed in Chapter 10. While accepting part of this argument (clawback would indeed be ineffective without tax changes), we need to ask whether the existing tax system was sacrosanct. Mr Barber has answered this question. His reductions in public expenditure have allowed him to cut the standard rate of tax. Whether he should have reduced taxation in this way (which, viewed in the context of the package as a whole, is upwardly redistributive) or by reducing the tax paid by those on lower incomes (which would have made room for clawback to operate) is of course a matter for political decision. It is therefore invalid to argue that the decision to introduce FIS was taken on purely *technical* grounds, because of the constraint imposed by the policies of the previous administration. It too was a *political* decision. The same broad considerations apply to the scale of the help provided. The Government has defended the £8 million benefits under FIS on the grounds that, when various offsets were taken into account, it provided more help than the £30 million increase in family allowances promised in the 1970 Budget Debate by the late Mr Iain Macleod. [165] To this, the answer is that Mr Macleod's £30 million is not sacrosanct either. If a family allowance increase were to leave large numbers of families below the poverty line then it too would be open to criticism. But here it is important to recognise that the failure of FIS to provide more help derives from a structural defect of FIS itself. The problem has been precisely stated by Sir Keith Joseph 'unless we forget the disincentive danger . . . and fill 100 per cent of the gap between a household's income and the make-up level, then automatically we shall be failing to reach the so-called poverty line'.[166] In other words, the logic of FIS has 'forced' him to set FIS benefits at a level which still leaves many families below the poverty line.

To take a broader long-term perspective, we can see that the strategy implicit in FIS is precisely that for which NIT was criticised. Poverty is seen as a remnant problem which can be solved by transferring the minimum of resources to those below a line. Ultimately, the debate between proponents of FIS (or NIT)-type solutions and most universalists is not over means (how an agreed objective is best achieved) but over ends (how much inequality we are prepared to tolerate).

7 *The role of family planning*

AUDREY SMITH

Family planning is defined here as the means whereby couples prevent or space births with the use of technical methods of contraception (i.e. oral, chemical and appliance methods) or by abstention outside the 'safe period' (rhythm method). The emphasis is deliberately on the methods of family planning that entail the acquisition of contraceptives or the seeking of professional advice. It is not possible, however, to include here two major methods: abortion and sterilisation.

Deciding which method to use, and ascertaining where and how to get it, is a problem for all parents, rich and poor alike. Every technical method has some disadvantages associated with it, whether in its actual use, or in the way it is obtained, or both. So couples try to work out which disadvantages they are most prepared to accept. Some couples have, however, a less rigorous concept of 'planning': many still prefer to 'risk it' or to use the less reliable methods of withdrawal or spasmodic abstention from sexual intercourse.

The course of action taken by any couple is influenced by a complex of rational and emotional thoughts. Parents can be helped or hindered by factors which are, to varying degrees, outside their control: their understanding of, and their aesthetic values regarding use of, different methods; how these methods work and how their bodies function in relation to them; their level of education; social class and income;[167] religious beliefs; sexual mores; and a variety of values that they may attach to the presence of children and, perhaps especially, of babies. Our different socialisation experiences give us different capacities to cope with the difficult problem of birth control.

This chapter considers the questions: how is family planning a bigger problem for the poor than it is for better-off members of our society; and how can the more effective use of technical methods relieve, to a greater extent than at present, the burden of poverty? In dealing with these questions, the essay draws heavily on a survey with which I am currently concerned.*

It must be stressed, however, that the association between poverty and family planning was only one aspect of the enquiry. Moreover, the survey was restricted to *large* families; and although large families are more likely to be poor, most poor families are not large.[168] Whether it is large or small, if a family is poor, additional children may be seen by the parents as another strain on their already limited resources. Not all the mothers whom I interviewed were currently in poverty; but many of them had known poverty in the past; and others had low incomes that offered only short-term security. It is the situation of these mothers, who have experienced both economic hardship *and* the problem of family planning, that has raised, in my mind, a number of questions about the efficacy of family planning in alleviating family poverty.

This essay is not intended to provide conclusive answers to those questions. It merely tries to show the nature of the problems that parents often experience in seeing family planning as a potential and acceptable means of easing their financial burdens. The obstacles are threefold: the attitudes of the parents; the methods of communicating information about family planning; and the attitudes of the advice-givers.

I shall first consider parental attitudes to various contraceptive methods, to family planning generally and to the economic burden of an additional child. In considering communications, we need not only to examine the general approach, but to ask whether and how couples obtain the method most suited to their

* At the time of writing, this investigation of a random sample of 100 mothers, residents in a northern city and having had six or more children, is nearing completion. The research has been supervised by Professor E. Grebenik, to whom the author is indebted for help in the preparation of this essay. This draws on only one aspect of the survey: the mothers' attitudes to their family size and to the use of birth control; the views of husbands, as reported by their wives, were also recorded. Pseudonyms are used in this report.

needs. Finally, what are the attitudes of the advice-givers to their role, especially with regard to poorer parents?

Parents' attitudes

Family planning provides a means to certain ends. The question 'How can we afford it?' has not only financial connotations: the emotional and physical ability to cope can be as important, if not more important, for some couples, than is the financial ability. This essay concentrates, however, on the economic liability aspect of family size. Although some parents will see family planning as a very welcome means of achieving a desirable end, others may reject this means either because the end is not desired or because seemingly insuperable obstacles stand between them and the desired end.

An improvement in one's standard of living, or at least the prevention of a reduction in it, is a desired end of families in all income brackets; but the poor have low aspirations.[169] Low incomes; insecurity of employment; inadequate housing; high rents; and low expectations of their children's chances of keeping up with the Joneses in the educational and financial rat-race, are some of the factors that lead, not surprisingly, to pessimism. Parents who feel that 'children keep you poor' are pointing to only one of many determinants in their situation. Some of these they entertain no hope of changing; but do they feel the same way about the number of children they have? Will another child be so great an addition to their financial burden? If they have low expectations of an improvement in their own standard of living and that of their children, another child may not be so big a set-back; but if they feel it is worth striving for even a small improvement, another child is likely to be seen as a disappointing, rather than a happy, event. As Mr Harding (one of the fathers who was present at an interview) said, 'I have a poor job. If I work 58 hours a week, it's not enough. We've as many as we can afford for the standard we want'. Mrs Harding added: 'If he does 76 hours a week, that's a good week and he's happy. He says every time I have a baby, he has to look for another job with a bit more money. And he has to work away for good money'.

For some couples, however, there are not such opportunities

to struggle against what is, for them, a treadmill and they may ask 'what's the point of bothering?' and tend to 'accept things as they come'. It is easy to dismiss such attitudes as 'fecklessness' or 'irresponsibility'; but as Coates and Silburn argue, people who wish to flog into conformity those who do not accept their stand-ards 'might make a plausible case if they could undertake to bear similar burdens in their own lives, and survive with any greater probity'.[170]

Bearing in mind these general observations, it is possible to distinguish four types of parental attitude that may restrict the use of family planning. It is not suggested that these categories are exhaustive or mutually exclusive. Comments made by some of the mothers illustrate the four categories:

(a) *The unconfident:* While fearing that another child will add to their financial problems, they feel unable to use birth control. Lack of confidence may result from a number of unsuccessful attempts or perhaps from the husband's unwillingness to co-operate. Ignorance about contraception generally or about the mechanics of a particular method, may lead to apprehension or even fear, Contraception, or a particular method, may be seen by some people as unreliable, by others as distasteful or taboo.[171] The experience of Mrs Dale illustrates some of these points:

I didn't want any more after two because we couldn't afford them. But it's what God gives you. I blame my husband; he wasn't careful [in withdrawing] and he says people still fall on when they take precautions, so it's a waste of time. We don't talk much about things like that.

Having 'fallen on' (become pregnant) when using the sheath, Mrs Dale finds the cap embarrassing and distasteful and dreads the prospect of the pill. Consequently, she relies on periodic abstinence and withdrawal; but having been told that not being able to afford it need no longer be an obstacle for people on low incomes, she is now contemplating the coil.

Mrs Butler explained why she was 'bitter and upset':

My husband thinks it's something you don't discuss. I took the pill, but it didn't agree with me; but I was determined this time. The doctor changed it three times. But he didn't seem as if he wanted to be bothered. He was so abrupt. I never went back. I persevered with the pill, but I got worried. It's a big thing for me to go to the doctor's. It would be too much for me to use the cap. To my generation it's all taboo to touch yourself.[172]

(b) *The ambivalent:* These mothers see positive advantages which override momentarily any thoughts of financial difficulties in having another child. While many parents experience such feelings, for these mothers it amounts to something of an obsession, and, like Mrs Cook, they may express deeply conflicting emotions:

> I didn't really want any more because of the money, but I wanted another when Catherine got past the baby stage. I've got more than I really wanted, but if I really hadn't wanted them, I'd have tried harder, wouldn't I? . . . It was my happy week when I 'came on', even when we used contraceptives. I could not get over the worry, no matter what we used. I didn't want any more after two, but I didn't really mind.

(c) *The antagonistic:* These mothers, who strongly oppose suggestions that they might use birth control, may or may not feel that another child will add significantly to their financial burden.

Mrs James felt that 'You should accept however many come. People nowadays don't. I think they are wrong. They are interfering with nature, with life itself. It leads to unhappiness. All this planning of families is wrong', and Mrs Atkinson agreed with her husband who believed that 'if God hadn't wanted you to have children, you wouldn't have had them. Those things [contraceptives] weren't made by God'. Mrs Machell thought that 'birth control is like murder. We think it's scandalous'.

The belief in the ruling force in one's life, of 'God', 'Nature' or 'Fate', is common among the antagonistic. It may be related to a religious commitment against birth control or to a mistrust, or even fear, of tampering with the bodily functions or with what is 'natural'.

(d) *The child-preferring group:* Another child is not seen as adding significantly to the family's difficulties, and so birth control is rejected. Mr and Mrs Spicer 'always say we can't afford them but when they come they are kept. I'm not put off by the money. That doesn't bother me. I go wild when I see little babies'. Mrs Finch reacted similarly: 'The money worries him more than it does me. If I knew my health would be O.K., I'd have one every year. I love kids'.

This fourfold classification is obviously an over-simplification of the attitudes expressed. For instance, a mother who prefers another child may also express antagonism or a lack of confidence about the use of birth control. Accepting the likelihood of another child or 'risking it' may be the easiest way out: she is choosing the least of the evils, and feels that this is the only acceptable solution to her dilemma. She and her husband may resort to less reliable, non-technical methods: more technical methods are too demanding an innovation. Recent research has shown that almost half the unskilled and semi-skilled couples use no birth control, and that the more reliable methods are used by the higher income groups.[173] One wonders how many couples, of all income groups, have turned to more reliable methods only after unwanted pregnancies; and how many of the poor, suffering from the sorts of inhibitions described above, manage to avoid having more children only by practising spasmodic abstinence or withdrawal? Many of us would feel that their 'quality of life' would be enhanced if they were able to use methods for which higher success rates are claimed. Unfortunately, the poor appear to be under more powerful pressures to contemplate such methods only as a last resort. The attitude of the male is important here. Reporting on their husbands' feelings, the survey wives spoke often of their opposition to male methods, while other men were hostile or indifferent to their wives' use of contraceptives.[174]

Obtaining family planning advice

Once parents have reached the point where they feel able to seek advice, a number of obstacles may thwart their attempts to obtain it. These obstacles are all the more awesome for those who had to overcome difficulties in their own attitudes or family situation and who seek advice in desperation. First, where to go? The chemist, the doctor, the family planning clinic, or the health visitor? The mother weighs up her feelings, which may be dominated by embarrassment or by fear of invasion of privacy.

Or she may wonder how to answer questions and be afraid of 'not knowing it all'. Mrs Mayhew expressed a common reaction:

> I've heard about the Family Planning Association. I don't think it's very nice to say to a perfect stranger: 'I've come about family planning'. You wonder who is going to look at what you say. They don't know you. It depends what kind of person you are and I am shy on things like that – going to clinics and being examined.

There may be practical problems of cost, even when the mother knows she can 'get it free'. As with the welfare benefits discussed in Chapter 2, free family planning may not be seen as a right. How accessible is the clinic or G.P.; and what can be done about minding the children? These difficulties can often amount to the last straw, as Mrs Clarkson explained:

> With the cap, I had to make an appointment and go to the other side of the city. It was a day's job to go. It did me in. I used it but I didn't get it replaced. It was a matter of fitting things in. I feel guilty about it. The help was available but you have to fit in the time.

The advice-givers

Three obstacles are considered under this heading: the professionals' concept, if any, of their role; the setting in which advice is offered; and the professionals' awareness of, and ability to tackle, the particular problems of poor clients.

There is a lack of consensus in the medical profession as to whether it is part of the G.P.'s role to give contraceptive advice. This involves such factors as ethical and religious objections; pressure of time; lack of relevant training; and a feeling that it is just not part of a doctor's role.[175] Even patients who have carefully chosen their doctor may find their access to family planning blocked by some of these factors. An unhelpful G.P. may be less of an obstacle, however, to patients who see a family planning service as their right. The barriers may be present, to varying degrees, when advice is sought, or hoped for, from other professionals, such as health visitors, midwives, nurses and social workers.[176]

G

The Family Planning Association is quite clear about its role; it is the setting in which it operates that gives rise for concern. The FPA is aware of the difficulties it faces in attracting lower socio-economic groups;[177] and, given its limited resources of staff and facilities, copes remarkably well. Many parents must find it difficult, however, to understand the overwhelming medical orientation of clinics. For parents who see family planning as a personal and emotional matter, facing the white-coated doctors and nurses may be frightening enough. Lay-workers who wear smocks in order to hand out pills and complete records may contribute further to the authoritarian atmosphere. A clinic-based organisation must inevitably find it difficult to overcome feelings of embarrassment, insecurity and suspicion. Domiciliary schemes have done something to break through these barriers; but it seems, from accounts so far,[178] that poor parents have a better chance of receiving this service if they can get themselves labelled 'problem' or even 'pre-problem' families.

An apparent over-concentration upon medical aspects and upon the role of the wife to the exclusion of the husband; and the use of middle-class vocabulary and media of communication seem more likely to exacerbate, than to alleviate, the problems of the poor. The wife who sees her difficulties as emotional ones, who wonders about her husband's likely reactions to various methods, and who doubts her ability to talk to him or get his sympathy, may feel that the advice-givers fail to appreciate her needs. Having come to terms with her feelings sufficiently to get to the clinic, she may find, when she arrives there, that these feelings are actually reinforced: the queuing may add to her embarrassment; the questions may remind her that she cannot speak 'like them'; and the physical examination may confirm her worst fears of being 'messed about with'. It may be the last straw when she has to pay for this privilege, because she is not deemed to be exempt.

In spite of the greater variety of female methods available, the popularity of the condom is easily understood. Although it means overcoming other objections, including the genital-touching taboo mentioned above, it is a way of avoiding doctors and clinics.

The National Health Service (Family Planning) Act, 1967, empowered local authorities in England and Wales to make arrangements for giving advice on contraception, and for the medical examination of those seeking advice, and to supply contraceptive substances and appliances. The Act extended the previous powers of local health authorities by making it possible for them to assist (or to arrange for other bodies, such as the FPA, to do so as their agents) persons who needed help on social grounds, and not only, as hitherto, in medical cases. The initial response has been disappointing; but by June 1971, 'only a handful of authorities [were] seriously falling down on the job'.[179] Obtaining advice is a problem for many parents; and the poor have unequal access to information and help. We need to question how far the system they have to combat affects their ability to accept family planning. It might lead us to think that more help, and of a different kind to that already existing, is called for.

Those intent on giving advice on family planning want to help. When confronted, however, by people who resent their form of help or the manner in which it is given, they may feel not only confused but indignant. The offer of help may be seen, by some parents, as interference. In attempting to solve one set of problems, those who offer help or advice on birth control may present the parents with new problems. Awareness of these difficulties can make the help more effective, but this makes considerable demands on time and other scarce resources.

Giving family planning help implies certain values about family life and the ethics of birth control. An appreciation of socio-cultural values and normative differences is called for. How far are we propagating, under the guise of enthusiasm for family planning, a personal, some might say middle class, morality about contraception, family size and standards of child-rearing? How do we view the question of freedom of choice regarding family size, when this may mean that some parents want or have more children than what we feel is good for them or for society?

We must accept that where family planning help is desired, we may have to reconsider the terms on which it is given in order that it be effective. Ability to do this may all too often be frustrated by financial limitations. We can only look forward to the day when this service becomes an integral part of the National Health Service.[180]

Family planning and the Child Poverty Action Group

Although its 1970 policy statement[181] makes no reference to
such a solution, CPAG has recognised, from the outset, that an
improvement in family planning facilities should form part of
a programme for tackling family poverty.[182] Some members have
argued, at conferences of the Group, that such measures should
play a more prominent part in the Group's platform; but the
emphasis has rightly remained on the major cause of family
poverty, low incomes. Such an emphasis has not been widely
appreciated in the FPA, at whose conferences family poverty is
discussed with inadequate attention to its causes. Implied or,
sadly, quite explicit, moral judgments about the child-bearing
behaviour of the poor are made, with little reference either to
their ability to make decisions about the spacing and frequency
of pregnancies or to *our* responsibility to improve the society
that moulds their attitudes and difficulties. As one who has
attended conferences of both organisations, I am disappointed
by the misunderstanding between them.[183]

Many of us believe that family planning can add immensely
to the quality of the lives of individuals and to society as a whole.
It can alleviate not only the poverty suffered by some of our
citizens, but it can take away, in all income groups, the worry
of unwanted pregnancies. Whatever its relevance to the *alleviation* of poverty, however, when we discuss the *causes* of poverty,
we need to turn to the more fundamental issue of unequal distribution of wealth and earned income.

8 Low pay: a case for a national minimum wage?

JOHN HUGHES

Within the field of pay policy, low pay is now being treated with a greater sense of urgency. As one aspect of the growing discussion of the direction that policy about low pay should take, there has been a revival of interest in the potential use of a statutory national minimum wage. This connects with the disillusion felt about the performance of the existing statutorily based system of wages councils. These were sharply criticised by, among others, the Donovan Commission, for their failure not only to raise the pay of lower paid workers, but even to secure suitable information on earnings and wage systems, to exercise control over actual pay (rather than minima), and to extend voluntary collective bargaining.[184] As only minor reforms in the wages council system are so far envisaged,[185] it is natural that attention as to the scope for statutory action should turn elsewhere. Besides, still in the field of initiative through statute, the commitment to 'equal pay' by 1975 demonstrates that bold statutory initiative can cut through a complex wages system with its inequalities and discrimination so far all too rigidly preserved. As the vast majority of women workers are low paid by any standard, it follows that a statute that strikes down discrimination between men's and women's wages has a profound direct impact on the present pattern of low pay. But the demonstration of the impact of legislation based on a more principled approach to pay inequalities must also quicken interest in a national minimum wage.

In examining the pros and cons of a national minimum wage one has first to identify some features in the recent revival of interest in low pay, the more so since these are associated with views on low pay policy which emphasise aspects other than a statutory national minimum. First, incomes policy with its declared concern for social justice at least found it necessary to accept some priority for the low paid. This, however, was a disappointment in practice; thus the TUC in its *Economic Review 1969* found, in a review of available statistics, no evidence of any significant improvement, and some evidence of relative worsening, in the position of the low paid.[186] It was also a disappointment in terms of a failure to achieve an adequate understanding of the nature of the problem; thus the PIB, by its Fourth General Report, had reached the ludicrously narrow view that 'except in a minority of instances . . . the improvement of the position of the low paid can be subsumed in the general problem of increasing efficiency'.[187] A further impetus to the examination of low pay policy has come from more detailed and critical studies of poverty, though the direction in which policy advocacy then moved was primarily towards altered tax and benefit incidence, i.e. working on the 'social wage' rather than on the wage structure itself.[188] Last, but by no means least, the Trades Union Congress, having recognised the limited impact of previous collective bargaining policy in achieving any relative improvement of the position of the low paid, has carried out the only comprehensive review yet attempted,[189] and has itself made suggestions embracing the 'efficiency' approach, the 'tax benefit' approach,[190] and statutory intervention. More recently, it is obviously moving towards a renewed interest in collective bargaining initiative, this time of a more co-ordinated and purposive kind.

Given the presence, and influential advocacy, of these other approaches to low pay (the efficiency approach; the tax/benefit approach; renewed collective bargaining initiatives), discussion of a statutory minimum wage has to be looked at in relation to the strength of these other methods.

The facts of low pay

But a statutory minimum has also to be based firmly on the

known facts about low pay. Fortunately, the growing concern about low pay has led to far better statistical information than was ever available before.[191] The statistics have in fact been better and more useful than the Government's attempt at analysis. The Department of Employment and Productivity has published a working party report, *A National Minimum Wage: An Enquiry*. Unfortunately, the result has been to create a misleading impression of the current costs of adopting particular levels of minimum wage. Nor did the working party develop any adequate economic analysis of the effects of a national minimum.[192]

It is possible to use the new earnings survey in conjunction with an earlier and more limited survey to examine what was the experience of low paid workers between 1960 and 1968.[193] None of this information suggests any significant relative improvement in the position of low paid workers; some of it indicates a deterioration. Thus :

1. For manufacturing as a whole, both manual men's and women's pay dispersions showed no change over the period 1960 to 1968 : in both these years weekly earnings of the *lowest decile* were 70 per cent of the *median* earnings for men, and 73 per cent for women. However, unchanged dispersion may conceal some relative deterioration, as there is evidence that a retail price index for low paid workers over this period would show a faster price rise than for higher paid workers.[194]

2. Outside manufacturing, the three largest industrial groups of *manual* workers whose earnings were surveyed in 1960 showed clear evidence of workers at the bottom end of the pay dispersion falling further behind. For men's earnings in *construction*, the lowest decile was 77 per cent of the median in 1960 but fell to 72 per cent by 1968; in *road passenger transport*, the fall was from 77 per cent to 71 per cent; in *local government*, the lowest decile fell from the high figure of 86 per cent of the median to 72 per cent by 1968. Thus a 'tail' of workers near the bottom of the pay dispersion was falling even further behind.

3. Over the same period, the industry with the lowest average earnings for men – agriculture – experienced a proportional rise in earnings considerably below the average for all industries.[195]

Turning to what the September 1968 earnings survey can tell us, it is revealing to take the earnings level widely used in discussion of a minimum wage, namely £15 a week gross pay. There is, in fact, an obvious difficulty in seeking to convey the scale of low pay by indicating how many fell below a particular line in hourly or weekly earnings at one moment in time. This is partly a difficulty in interpreting the statistics themselves.[196] It is partly that the numbers falling below a particular threshold level of gross pay will, in our inflationary economy, fall dramatically in number as time goes on. Thus, I estimate that, in September 1968, there were 1 million men in full time work with weekly earnings under £15, and 2 million with weekly pay under £17. But by mid 1970, my estimate is that approximately 450,000 were earning under £15 gross, and 1 million under £17 gross per week. This sort of numbers game has to be borne in mind when we go on to deal with the alleged cost of a minimum wage, or with the proportion of workers it would affect. Thus, a £17 minimum in mid-1970 would have affected only the same proportion of men as a £15 minimum back in September 1968.

Of our 1 million men in September 1968 earning less than £15 gross, 840,000 were manual workers, 160,000 non-manual. As to women workers, there were 3,875,000 approximately earning under £15 gross per week (2.2 million manual; 1.675 million non-manual). In percentage terms, 8 per cent of full-time men earned under £15, but 70 per cent of full-time women.[197] Over a quarter of full-time women workers (approximately 1.44 millions) earned under £10 a week gross. In terms of working out a policy, these earnings differences as between men and women are extremely important. So it is worth burdening the reader with a further salient statistic. These are available from the DEP figures of hourly earnings for manual workers excluding overtime premia. These show median hourly earnings for men as £0.44½ and for women £0.27; at the lowest decile, manual men's hourly earnings are £0.33 and women's £0.20½.

What the September 1968 figures also show are the occupations, industries, age groups and regions most affected by a high proportion of low paid workers. Since we are going on to assess the economic implications of a national minimum wage these characteristics are important. Thus:

1. Over half the manual working men earning under £15 were aged 50 and over. (These older age groups are also par-

ticularly affected by economic insecurity in the form of high unemployment rates).

2. Certain regions in the country have relatively high proportions of low paid workers; their labour markets are also characterised by high rates of unemployment and net migration of labour. Thus lower quartile earnings of men were £20 in the more prosperous South East and West Midlands, but only about £17.50 in Scotland and the South Western region and £18 in the Northern region, Yorkshire and Wales.

3. Certain industries have high proportions of low paid workers. These are not exclusively the small firm, small establishment, industries where wages councils operate; but it is significant that lower quartile earnings for manual men in Wages Council industries were only £15.15 compared with £18.10 as lower quartile earnings in 'all industries and services'. A number of the industries and services in which there are high proportions of low paid manual men are in the public sector of employment (including public administration, and the educational and health services). Thus, neither public employment nor the operation of statutory wages orders appear to afford any guarantees against the prevalence of low pay – not so far, at any rate. Yet these are areas where a deliberate re-direction of state policy could have direct and tangible influence.

And a national minimum wage?

The most directly challenging way to ask the state to step in and improve the position of low paid workers is through the agency of some form of national minimum wage. This has the attraction also of being immediately understood by the workers that it would affect; one might assume that consequently enforcement would be administratively simpler than in the case of the complex pattern of Wages Council orders which have done so little, anyway, to level up the lowest paid trades.

How much could be claimed for a national minimum would, of course, depend on where it was pitched and what proportion of the labour force – overall and in particular areas and industries – received direct pay increases as a result. Potentially, it 'would be a useful tool for achieving social justice by providing more comprehensive protection against exploitation than exists at present'; it 'would contribute to the relief of poverty amongst employed people and in so doing would reduce the problem of the wage stop'.[198] There is some force too in the argument that it would encourage increased efficiency in labour use, though there would be no direct *bargained* connection between statutory minimum pay and the performance of workers.

Given the variations of weekly hours from one industry to another, and given too the complexity of many pay structures and the varying relationships between 'basic' pay and earnings, the inter-departmental working party came to the conclusion that a national minimum had best be expressed in *hourly* terms and as a minimum *earnings* guarantee.[199] This is probably the most useful approach to adopt at this stage, though it may leave relatively unaided many aspects of pay (such as overtime rates, holiday pay, etc.) which are geared to lower 'basic' rates. We can accept too the working party suggestion that we can best think of an 'acceptable' weekly national minimum by assuming a 40 hour week – as the most widely spread 'normal' week – when deriving a suitable hourly rate (for example: £15 for 40 hours; £0.37½ an hour), but guaranteeing a standard minimum for all normal hours.

The apparent simplicity of this approach to low pay quickly disappears, however, when we examine the real tests that a statutory minimum has to meet. In brief, the approach could only hope to achieve moderate success if it were part of a complex strategy designed to deal with low pay through a *number* of instruments of economic management.

(*a*) *The 'cost' of a national minimum wage:* the working party made estimates of cost which seem to have done more to confuse the issue than clarify it. This was in part because they had only very limited information to work on as to pay dispersion (what was available from the Family Expenditure Survey), and the approximate period of time to which their annual cost estimates relate is not set down clearly but apparently relates to spring 1968 to spring 1969. Thus they concluded that the *direct* cost of a £0.37½ minimum for men and a £0.25 minimum for women would be an increase in annual pay of £560 million. Much more reliable data are now available as to pay dispersion, including hourly pay of manual workers excluding overtime premia. Thus the working party's figures require complete re-calculation and up-dating to indicate the present day 'cost' of particular levels of minimum wage. My own estimate, using methods similar to those of the working party[200] is that in the year spring 1969 to spring 1970 the direct 'cost' of a minimum earnings guarantee of £0.37½ an hour for men and £0.25 an hour for women would have been only a little over £200 million (or an increase of less than 1 per cent on the total wage and salary bill). For the calendar year 1970 the direct 'cost' of such minima would probably be around £150 million. One sees here the effect of thinking of a given minimum at different periods of time. What is serious is that much of the interest in a national minimum has been killed off because the working party's calculations have been taken as a reliable indicator of the *current* cost of applying specific levels of national minima. Even the TUC's document, *Low Pay*, published in February 1970, estimates only that the working party report's figures should be halved; in fact they should be scaled down even more heavily.

Of course, a further element in the cost implications of a national minimum wage concerns the effect of such a minimum upon differentials. This question of differentials deserves separate treatment, especially as it is not realistically pursued in the official study. But let us suppose that a national minimum is fixed at a level that does directly raise the pay of many low paid workers (my £200 million p.a. calculation in the previous paragraph would directly raise the pay of about 2 million manual men and women). Assume besides that there are extensive enough effects on differentials to treble the total cost of such a policy. What problems of economic management does this involve?

(*b*) *Some economic consequences of a national minimum wage:* First of all, it might be argued that the statutory requirement to increase pay sharply to bring it up to a defined minimum would have adverse employment consequences for the very workers the policy sets out to help. This consideration should not simply be brushed aside, but the scale of the problem should not be exaggerated. Indeed, Selective Employment Tax (SET) has created, since 1966, an equivalent effect (in terms of costs to employers and, therefore, their attitude to employment) to a phased introduction of a minimum wage. In the services sector of the economy we have therefore been getting the employment and 'efficiency' effects of a 'high wage' economy while still, alas, perpetuating a system of low pay for masses of workers. This change has gone through against a background of general economic management involving higher unemployment, and without any specific protection being afforded to workers in the services sector. Thus we should not be frightened away from advocacy of a national minimum on employment grounds since SET has already demonstrated that the employment problem created by a rise in unit labour costs is a limited one; but we should demand suitable accompanying measures. The 'suitable measures' include running the economy at a generally high level of activity and employment and being ready to reduce selectively the rates of SET or of the proposed Value Added Tax (VAT) in order to offset the possible threat to employment levels generated by the combined upward pressure of SET, 'equal pay' and potential minimum wage requirements. Insofar as *older* workers might be more exposed to employment consequences than others, there should either be introduced a quota system for the employment of older workers, or SET could be remitted (for instance on workers aged over 55).

The employment problem has a specifically *regional* aspect. As there are proportionately more low paid workers in certain regions (largely involving the Development Areas), the rise in the total pay bill would be greater proportionately in those regions. *If* we could prevent costs rising, there would be a beneficial effect, in those regions, from higher real pay and higher effective demand. But if the cost of the minimum wage is not offset, then at least some of the cost increase would affect the competitive strength of certain industries in such regions and might have adverse employment implications. This might be particularly serious for the employment prospects of older workers. And some at least of the cost of the minimum wage might be passed on in higher prices within such regions and thereby reduce the real wage improvement. To offset the cost increase in such regions would require regionally selective reductions in SET rates rather than their general reduction or abolition. Alternatively, this situation points to the need for the maintenance, or indeed the extension, of the Regional Employment Premium.

The need for 'offsets' to prevent the cost of a minimum wage being transmitted through into higher consumer prices is glaringly obvious when we consider the implications for food prices. Agriculture, food manufacturing, and distribution, are all services with high proportions of low paid workers;[201] consequently their costs would rise disproportionately if a minimum wage were instituted, and the cumulative effect of this could be transmitted into food prices – with its obviously adverse effects on all low income households (including pensioner households unaffected by the improvement in pay). Again, a deliberate policy of 'offsetting' would be required. This might entail higher agricultural subsidies; SET could be removed from, or at least reduced in, the food distributive trades; while VAT might be introduced only at a lower rate, or not at all, in these industries.

All of these measures may, in fact, represent intelligent steps in a policy aimed at the improvement of the conditions of the low paid. They might rationally be advocated (e.g. the removal of SET from the food trades) even in the absence of a minimum wage policy. But notice how the apparent simplicity of the attack on poverty through the administrative device of a minimum wage has become only one element in a complex economic strategy.

(c) *Implications, for a statutory minimum, of 'equal pay' and differentials:* The 'equal pay' legislation means that any government, between now and 1975, would consider the level and the phasing of a national minimum in relation to the time-table for 'equal pay' and *its* impact on costs. If we presume that the legislation on equal pay rules out any differentiation in national earnings minima as between men and women after 1975, then a number of consequences follow. As has been indicated earlier the differences in average hourly earnings of men and women are so great that a shift to a common minimum would either involve pitching that at such a low level as to affect very few men or it would lead to a violent increase in the hourly earnings of a very high proportion of women. There is no escaping this logic, and it is likely to harden the resistance of the government to a national minimum wage. To put it another way, the main beneficiaries from a national minimum would be women workers, and it might indeed have more dramatic implications for women's pay than 'equal pay' itself. (One example, to demonstrate, assuming a £0.35 hourly earnings in mid-1970 is equivalent to the £0.30 level back in September 1968, a £0.35 hourly minimum now would affect only three per cent of manual men but 65 per cent of manual women.)

The other aspect of differentials that has to be faced is this: a number of low paid industries have narrow pay dispersions anyway. Consequently, one could not ask that workers in such industries should be levelled up to the minimum if below it, but should not have their pay increased if above it. For instance, in September 1968, 78 per cent of men farmworkers were below £0.35 an hour. Suppose a £0.35 minimum had been introduced; it is unthinkable that three-quarters of the men in an entire industry could have been stuck on the minimum. The whole pay structure – which offers all too little prospects of higher earnings as it is – would have to move up. This would be true of any industry or service with a high proportion of its workers below the minimum. If extended repercussions on the whole pay structure of the country are to be avoided (and if they occurred it would be difficult to improve the *real* pay of the lowest paid) a minimum wage policy would have to have the active support of the TUC and would have to involve some guarantees that organised unions in industries with higher average wages would accept the catching up process of pay in industries with low average wages.

This requirement of trade union co-operation, of the disciplined co-ordination of trade union response, is a real one. Once again, it destroys the notion of a simple administrative device.

The nature of our pay system is such that it will require the conscious co-operation of organised trade unionism if any major realignment of pay structures in favour of the lower paid is to occur. One can only avoid this conclusion by pitching a national minimum wage so low that it has only derisory significance as a weapon of social policy. At the moment, the use of statute to push through 'equal pay' has created a situation complex enough but with a substantial measure of trade union co-operation. As the trade union movement is only now turning to a co-ordinated study of the wider question of low pay, it is not possible to say in advance how far disciplined co-operation in pay policy to advance the conditions of the low paid will be forthcoming.

(*d*) *Minimum wage and the tax structure:* As argued above, a strategy for the introduction of a minimum wage would need to include a flexible re-arrangement of the existing structure of employment taxes and subsidies. It is worth emphasising a further aspect. The object of a national minimum is clearly to improve the real disposable income of the lowest paid. But as the government's studies of the incidence of taxes show, at these low levels of earned income a high proportion of incremental income is subject to direct and indirect taxation. The proportion varies with composition of household, but it might be put at about a third of incremental income absorbed in taxation.[202] Thus, if the desired results of a national minimum wage are to be achieved, that is a *real income improvement concentrated on workers previously below the minimum,* it would be rational for the government to alter the incidence of taxation and benefits at low levels of earned income. In this way, any given national minimum would have more impact in improving real income where it is intended to. Thus we should not see the approach to low household income through the incidence of taxes and benefits and the approach through a minimum wage policy as separate issues.

The need for a wider strategy

Perhaps the upshot of this whole argument is that, in demanding statutory intervention to precipitate improvements in the position of low paid workers, we cannot bypass the real social and economic complexities underlying low pay. This is not an argument against statutory intervention; indeed it may be (as with 'equal pay') that only statutory power can ensure a radical enough assistance to the low paid. But the state initiative when it comes has to incorporate the additional elements of taxation strategy, of collective bargaining policy, and of economic management that are all required. Thus, for instance, the possibly damaging consequences on employment prospects of either or both 'equal pay' and national wage minima are greater in under-employed labour markets (such as we have experienced since 1967) than if economic management steers closer to full employment. Against these real requirements, the standard 'problems' of a national minimum wage, such as the criteria for its periodic re-calculation, appear relatively insignificant. (Thus the best approach to the revision of the minimum is to relate it periodically to median earnings; e.g., say, 70 per cent of the median).

That being so, one is tempted to re-consider building a statutory minimum wage policy from a revamped system of wages councils. If these were given the task of achieving earnings and conditions broadly comparable to those in unionised industries, encouraging the development of trade union organisation and collective bargaining systems within their sectors, and were given at least some resources for improving the levels of efficiency in labour utilisation in their sectors, there might be hope. A re-grouping into larger, 'sectoral' wages councils, and the development of some central wages council with supervisory powers and expert services, would then help to align minimum rates in the direction of a common national minimum with statutory powers of enforcement. It would be better than the feebleness and lack of direction exhibited at present; after all, here are *existing* statutory wage fixing bodies. Why not give them a strategy and some real bite?

9 Children's allowances: an economic and social necessity

SIR JOHN WALLEY

No social provision is so widely misunderstood in our country as family allowances. Yet we might have pioneered them as long ago as 1796! The circumstances, which have been widely ignored or misrepresented in our history books, are worth recalling because they establish the essential case for such allowances which, since the 1914-18 War, has been accepted by every industrial country – for we may now include President Nixon's Family Assistance Programme.[203]

Historical background: a false dawn

Before the industrial and agricultural revolutions, children, free from school, helped their parents in the home-based industries of the time or could be apprenticed. Even so, the poor law sometimes paid allowances to workers 'overburdened with young children'.[204] Before the French war, children were becoming much more of a financial burden, especially in agricultural workers' families hit by the effects of enclosures as well as by the competition of factory production. The war brought further hardships and there was a run of bad harvests. In 1795, the Berkshire magistrates introduced the 'Speenhamland System' – a form of minimum income guarantee using the local poor-rate to make up earnings to amounts determined by the price of bread and the number of children.[205] The magistrates were practical men trying to protect the poor in a war emergency and their

H

action was generally approved and imitated. In Parliament, the Whigs had another idea: Whitbread's Bill for an agricultural minimum wage. Academic historians still sometimes suggest that this was the 'right' remedy,[206] ignoring both the case developed against it, and the alternative offered, by the Prime Minister and Chancellor of the Exchequer, William Pitt. He argued that an admittedly bad situation could be remedied neither by a poor law which prevented a family moving in search of better conditions and compelled it to be destitute before it could be helped, nor by a wage system which took no account of family responsibilities:

> Were the minimum fixed upon the standard of a large family, it might operate as an encouragement to idleness on one part of the community; and if it were fixed on the standard of a small family, those would not enjoy the benefit of it for whose relief it was intended. What measures then could be found to supply the defect? Let us make relief in cases where there are a number of children a matter of right and an honour, instead of a ground for opprobrium and contempt.[207]

Pitt promised to bring in a Bill to give effect to his ideas and Whitbread, giving up his, particularly commended the idea of family allowances. If Pitt had limited himself to his proposed allowances of one shilling for each child beyond the second (beyond the first for widows) and his general poor law reforms, he might well have succeeded, but his zeal outran his discretion and his Bill covered even more ground than did the Beveridge Report.[208] For children, there was to be comprehensive industrial schooling; for adults, work or maintenance if unemployed; and for sickness and old age, a system of subsidised general contributory insurance. Even the genius of Pitt could not, in an increasingly menacing war situation, get such a vast and unpractical programme further than the approval of a House of Commons Committee.[209] But Pitt's concern for children did not stop at family allowances. The income-tax[210] which he pioneered two years later included a system of allowances for children which was more sophisticated than our own: they increased with, but more slowly than, the parents' total income. These were swept away following Pitt's death in 1806 and were not revived for more than a hundred years.

For anything approaching Pitt's general clarity of thought about the basic social requirements of a modern society, the country would have to wait until it had gone through the traumatic experience of another general war. The blind reaction to Speenhamland which produced the 1834 Poor Law Commission set out to solve our problem by simply abolishing cash relief for the able-bodied worker and his family. To be helped they must split up and go into one of the 'Bastilles', as the new workhouses were soon dubbed. The resultant absence of any tolerable social security for the worker may go far to explain the nineteenth-century growth of population which the 'reformers' had wanted to discourage: one could now only look to one's children for support in widowhood, disablement and old age. Contraceptives may not, after all, be a sufficient answer to the 'population explosion' in countries which are as innocent of social security as they are of family allowances.

Family allowances accepted

While one line of nineteenth-century reform was insisting that the welfare of children was no concern of the State, another, inconsistently, by compulsory schooling and the prevention of child employment, put obligations on parents without providing them with help in discharging them. The effect was seen in the reports of social investigators (and of the recruiting sergeants for the South African War) which, in 1905, led to the inauguration of the Welfare State with a modest measure for school meals.[211] Lloyd George brought back income-tax allowances for children in his 1909 budget, but the benefits of the schemes of social insurance on which he and Churchill were already embarked were seen only as compensation for lost earnings and, like them, ignored family responsibilities. This remained the position in health insurance until 1948 but, in the reconstruction of unemployment insurance which followed the 1914-18 war, the benefit took the 'subsistence' shape which Beveridge would later apply to the whole of our social security. This was no doubt influenced by the rates of 'outdoor relief' to which the Poor Law had been forced, by rising unemployment, to resort; but a powerful impulse also came (via the 'out-of-work donation' of the demobilisation period) from the family allowances which had been introduced into the pay of the Forces during the war. These, too, had been a long time on the road : Wellington had asked for them for his troops in the Peninsular Campaign.

For the first time in our history, a man with a family might now be financially better off without work. Eleanor Rathbone quickly drew the moral in her still thought-provoking book, *The Disinherited Family*,[212] which, in 1924, built up an overwhelming case for introducing children's allowances. She had no temptation to suggest that such allowances would increase the birthrate. Heavy unemployment had created a belief that the country was overpopulated and it was only in official circles that warnings were being given about the need for young people to support the country's threatening future burden of old-age dependency. Her case was strictly economic and social. In Australia, she could point to a Royal Commission which, in 1919, had advised that a minimum wage adequate to the needs of the three-child family, beloved of wage negotiators, would absorb more than the total national product! The Commission's Chairman had then suggested that if only *actual* children were paid for, employers would have no difficulty in meeting the cost through an employment levy. In France, Germany and neighbouring countries, there had been a big development of children's allowances as part of wages; this had enlisted the support of trade unions, though governments were not involved. In all these cases the aim was to secure a better distribution of wages so that workers with children not only got more but got it when they needed it. In Britain, Eleanor Rathbone had the further argument that our unemployment payments would otherwise deprive many workers of the incentive to keep or accept employment while they had children. Substituting supplementary for unemployment benefit, this is still the easiest way of presenting the case for family allowances in Britain, but it was the continental argument which nearly gave Eleanor Rathbone a sensational victory. The 1925 Samuel Commission on the Coal-mining Industry[213] recommended children's allowances as the only way of reconciling a living wage for the miner with the industry's competitive position. Beveridge (along with Keynes, an early convert) was a member of the Commission but the hard fact behind the recommendation was that such allowances were being paid by the industry's continental competitors. If Baldwin had succeeded in his efforts to secure all-round acceptance of the Commission's recommendations as a package-deal we might, in 1926, have had children's allowances instead of the General Strike and the tragic coal-mining stoppage which dragged on after it. The miners were among Eleanor Rathbone's warmest supporters in the long campaign on which she was now embarked.

The belief that family allowances come from the Beveridge Report is mistaken; Churchill's War Coalition government had already announced that they would accept them if they had TUC support, and this came at the 1942 Congress. While the Government was probably thinking of them as a contribution to wage restraint, the Beveridge Report, which came later in that year, naturally insisted on their social security and 'incentive' aspects:

> It is dangerous to allow benefit during unemployment or disability to equal or exceed earnings during work . . . The gap between income during earning and during interruption of earning should be as large as possible for every man. It cannot be kept large for men with large families, except either by making their benefit in unemployment and disability inadequate, or by giving allowances for children in time of earning and not earning alike.[214]

Most unfortunately, in his March 1943 broadcast on postwar reconstruction, Churchill cited the widespread alarm about the declining birthrate and the need to encourage 'our people . . . by every means to have large families' to explain the 'prime importance' that he attached to 'well-thought-out plans for helping parents to contribute this lifespring to the community'.[215] This could explain why the 1945 Family Allowances Act was the only 'Beveridge' measure to become law under the War Coalition Government. Parliament then only wanted more: either payment for the first child or, more insistently, the £0.40 Beveridge rate instead of the £0.25 proposed. The Government said the latter was to leave room for more benefits in kind and promised free school-meals for all.[216] The Attlee Government's decision to make £0.37½ the rate for the first child (without anything extra for other children) in the 1946 National Insurance Act suggested that a corresponding change in the family allowance rate would soon follow. But, before 1968, the only general increase was that to £0.40 in the Conservatives' first (1952) budget, specifically to counter the effect on families of abolishing the bread subsidy. In 1956, a further £0.10 was added for children after the second; this was associated with rising concern about dietary deficiencies in larger families. The value of the original £0.25 has been restored since 1968,[217] but the promise on which it rested is forgotten. The payments for children in social security benefits therefore continue to be so much larger than family allowances that we are still wrestling with a situation in which very many children are having to live below our 'subsistence' minimum simply *because* their parents are in regular work. A country's concern for its future is shown in its care for its children. Clearly something has gone badly wrong with the programme which evoked such an enthusiastic war-time response.

The population question

The economic and social case for children's allowances is stronger today than when Beveridge wrote. We are applying to join the EEC whose members know their value, and we have the new legal obligation to establish equal pay by 1975, with all its implications for the family. We also have the growing pressure on poor parents to enable their children to 'keep up with the Joneses' in our socially undifferentiated schools and other organisations.

The big adverse factor has been the change-round in popular and official attitudes on the population question. Given our present demographic structure and the ease with which our young people can emigrate, some current views on population seem about as rational as those which, when Eleanor Rathbone started her campaign, would have deprived us of the young people who saw us through the war and are now working to support our very large, and still increasing, number of pensioners. Churchill's 1943 use of the 'dwindling birthrate' argument may have a lot to do with the widespread belief that family allowances promote births and, by an easy transition (perhaps prompted by the association with social security), more births to irresponsible parents. There is singularly little evidence to suggest

that they have had either effect anywhere.[218] France is famous
for its big allowances but its birthrate is below that of the USA
which has, so far, paid none; Canada's birthrates have always
moved in close sympathy with those of its neighbour, and the
introduction of family allowances did not disturb the pattern;
in Czechoslovakia, a falling birthrate over a long period has
gone hand in hand with improving family benefits; while
Sweden is notable both for its family benefits and for one of
the lowest birthrates in the world. These facts should surprise
no one. Nowhere have children's allowances tried to cover anything like the cost of having and caring for a child. The idea
that anyone in this country would embark on this for our average payment of £0.55 per child per week or even for many
times that amount is absurd.

I would agree, if the suggestion was that a more appreciative
public attitude here to those who undertake the heavy responsibilities of bringing up children might help us to retain some
who now emigrate; but those who complain about 'over-popula-
tion' are quite as likely to complain about the 'brain drain'. As
for irresponsible parenthood, children's allowances mean correspondingly smaller social security payments. The real beneficiaries
of increased family allowances are responsible citizens in regular
work; all that the shiftless and irresponsible get from them is a
better incentive to be less shiftless and more responsible. Because
this is so, people who have studied the facts have argued that
improved children's allowances may even *reduce* birthrates.[219]

Family allowances and taxation

Family allowances, though paid universally, have never benefited
the well-to-do. The only recognition of children in our income
and surtax systems is the flat-rate allowances for them. These
neither provide a cash benefit for children, as is sometimes
suggested, nor, except marginally, reduce tax rates: they simply
exempt from taxation the income required for bare subsistence.
It is, therefore, entirely logical to adjust them to take account
of family allowances. Chancellors have generally been shy to
admit to any relationship between the two kinds of child allowance but the coming of family allowances enabled Governments
to hold the child tax-allowance at its pre-war rate of £60 until

1952, and, for family allowance children under 11, it was only £13 more in 1970-71. (Although the tax allowance was £115, 'clawback' entailed a reduction, in total tax allowances, of £42 : see Chapter 10.) Clawback, which came as an unwelcome surprise in 1968 to taxpayers with families (and which, if account is also taken of the increased charge for school meals and the withdrawal of welfare milk which formed part of Mr Gordon Walker's 'package',²²⁰ was largely responsible for bringing down to less than £50 million the cost of family allowance increases whose face value was £183 millions), was only necessary because family allowances had been stagnant for so long. Going back to 1945, most tax-payers with families have lost rather than gained from the coming of family allowances. Those who resist the clawback should be questioning, instead, the failure of our income and surtax systems to deal equitably with marriage and family responsibilities at *all* income levels. The fact that, unlike other countries, we tax family allowances is another legitimate grievance. A child is not less expensive to keep because its parents are better off. Finally, if governments are going to treat family, social security, and tax allowances for children as interchangeable, we ought not to tolerate a situation where an increase of the tax rate now makes the first smaller, has no effect on the second, and increases the value of the third.

The unpopularity of family allowances

I have suggested that two popular views about family allowances are mistaken. But why have they obtained such a hold? Paradoxically, the priority accorded to family allowances during the war may be one explanation. It deprived them of the understanding which comes from the public discussion of controversial measures. It also left them isolated from the less novel national insurance and national assistance legislation for which a big government publicity campaign was launched long after family allowances had started. Even the incentive argument was not clear at a time when unemployment was no more than a memory and sickness benefit still ignored dependants altogether. Beveridge had made family allowances no more than an 'assumption' of general government policy in his Report.²²¹ Their appearance in the social security budget put them – a payment to people in work – in apparent conflict with the needs of the old, etc. It also divorced them from government policies in the fields of taxation, incomes and wages, education, housing and rent control and the like: their use, in 1952, to ease out the bread subsidy was an isolated exception. That the original £0.25 rate was a compromise which could not be related to the social security structure or anything else was another disadvantage; compromises are always difficult to explain and this one was associated with unfulfilled promises.

It is perhaps not surprising that, with these presentational difficulties, family allowances soon became the forgotten item not only of government, but of party, politics, and that the increases of 1968 came only as a seemingly reluctant response to mounting evidence[222] of the extent to which children were forced to live below the subsistence level approved by Parliament.

Need for new approach

I have asked myself whether we have now to deal with a simple failure of political communication which can be put right by better explanations and publicity or whether we also need to break away from the system of family allowances recommended by Beveridge and seek a better way of enlisting public support for policies which will effectively end not only the scandal of child poverty in our midst but that of parents without the economic incentive to work for their betterment. I believe that we are faced with such a situation and that the whole idea of providing allowances, not for children directly but for 'the benefit of the family as a whole', and concentrating this help on the larger families because these are the ones most likely to be in poverty has been a great mistake. How can such an arrangement be said to help children when nothing at all is paid for more than half of them?* Especially today, people resent the preferential treatment of big families in the disbursement of public funds and are increasingly suspicious of helping 'poor' families which they cannot identify with those of people regu-

---

* Family Allowances are not paid to parents having only one child or only one dependent child. In other families, no payment is made for the eldest dependent child. This results in the exclusion of more than seven million children.

larly employed at trade union wages : we need something, free
from these presentational difficulties, which is based on an idea
simple enough to catch people's imaginations. Nor do we want
to be held up for the creation of some vast new, and probably
quite impossible, piece of government machinery such as 'negative income tax'.[223] My own answer[224] is that we should scrap
family allowances altogether and, following the example of other
countries, pay instead a *tax-free* allowance for every child ('child
endowment') which would be the same for all or could be varied
in the same age bands as present tax allowances. The existing
family allowances machinery would be adapted to pay it and its
rate (or rates) would be firmly tied in with earnings and social
security levels; but the cost would, like that of the tax allowances it replaced, be treated as a charge on the general revenue.
Child endowment would be explained as society's contribution
towards the heavy costs (many of them imposed by law) which
must nowadays fall on anyone caring for one of our future
citizens. It would be paid for the benefit of every child to who-
ever had the charge of it (jointly where parents were living
together).

This is not a case for sending a boy on a man's errand. The
child endowment must, from the start, be big enough to replace
completely not only the family allowances but the increases for
children now paid with the ordinary national insurance benefits
and the child tax-allowances of the standard rate taxpayer. To
achieve this our present average family allowance payment of
£0.55 per child would have to go up to £1.85. But as FIS would
not be needed, the *net* cost cannot be very much more than that
of abolishing clawback and the present taxation of family allowances – simplifications which would bring the 1971 average value
of a taxpayer's combined allowances very near to £1.85 per
child. The proper cost comparison is not with conventional
'government' spending, but with the big tax concessions, in recent
budgets, to working adults and with, say, $\frac{1}{2}$ per cent of the
national wages bill.

A revolutionary change

It will be a great mistake to seek to assess the cost or effects of
my proposal as if it had no dynamic of its own. For those on

social security benefits there might be little apparent change except where payments are now restricted by the 'wage stop'. This should be abolished since its only effect would then be on disabled people with abnormally low earnings which ought to be supplemented. It is, however, reasonable to assume that the new incentive to parents not only to accept but to seek and hold regular employment would reduce the numbers receiving unemployment payments. A special group is that of deserted mothers and women with illegitimate children now living on supplementary benefit who would see new possibilities of being self-supporting in work as well as in marriage (or re-marriage or even the return of an errant husband) when these things did not mean the loss of the payments for their children. Re-marriage might also be easier for widowed mothers when it did not mean giving up the payments for their children, as well as their own benefit.

For those in regular work, the immediate beneficiaries would be those whose earnings do not make them liable for tax. But, again, we must not overlook the financial savings as well as social benefits from the support which child endowment would bring to marriages now strained or actually broken in the desperate struggle to bring up children and keep a home together with no more help than our present family allowances. More easily quantifiable savings will come in the wide field of allowances and services now providing for families on a test of means : free school meals, school maintenance grants and rate rebates are outstanding examples.

Administration and the effect on our tax structure

Child endowment would add some three millions to the payments load of the family allowances administration but the work would be much easier because the composition of the child's family would not affect title. The administration of unemployment and sickness benefits would also be much simplified.

The Inland Revenue would be relieved of the whole business not only of taxing family allowances but of dealing with entitlement to child tax-allowance, for the efficient checking of which they are clearly not equipped − another source of very big savings from my proposal. Some kind of compensation would need to be arranged for surtax payers with children who would lose on the deal and something would no doubt have to be done about marginal cases such as university students and people with families abroad. But the really big effects would be as follows:

1. There would be a *reduction* in the number of assessments to be made (because child endowment would be tax free) but an *increase* in the numbers of parents liable to pay tax on additional income. This does not seem objectionable, since those concerned would now have the means to pay, and parents are less likely than most to be deterred from increasing their earnings by the thought of having to pay tax on them. But the numbers actually paying could also be less than before if arrangements were made for child endowment to be set against tax liability.

2. The tax machinery would be greatly simplified and the Inland Revenue relieved of a lot of work but it would then be immediately apparent that, unlike those of other countries, our tax rates are unprogressive and take no account of the taxpayers' family responsibilities; and also, perhaps, that our whole tax approach to the married relationship is hopelessly out-of-date and prejudicial to the family. For those whose concern is for children, a particularly objectionable feature is the total loss of the standard adult personal allowance suffered by women who give up work to care for their children.

Not the least of the advantages which I see from child endowment is the spotlight it must bring to bear on the deficiencies of our socially, as well as administratively, antiquated income tax system and the opportunity its easements would give for absorbing changes which social and economic principles have long since dictated in other countries.

The wages structure

I have emphasised the connection between children's allowances and the wages structure and how the TUC supported their introduction. This support has continued and the TUC has increasingly pressed for a big increase in family allowances. In recent *Economic Reviews* they have shown their interest in my proposal.[225] The Wilson Government may have missed a great opportunity by failing to make imaginative action of this sort a part of their search for an effective incomes policy. The cost of child endowment would have been almost trifling in relation to that of some of the inflationary wage increases they had to accept and the pressures for which will get a further impetus as we move towards the date for legal enforcement of equal pay unless we start by taking the children out of the firing line. A system of equal, untaxed payments for all the nation's children is obviously a very much better base for a rational structure of wages and incomes generally than our present confusion of allowances. With adequate child endowment there should also be no need for special protection of the 'lower paid' which (because it is undifferentiated) is so often merely the springboard for general advances, in the consequences of which children may well be the chief sufferers.

Conclusion

Child endowment is much more than a device for relieving child poverty – important as that is. I see it as the beginning of a much needed re-examination of national policies on a very wide front which should enlist support from all sorts of people on whose minds the statistics of child poverty have made little impression. Have not the poor been always with us? In a campaign for child endowment there must clearly be the closest possible co-operation with the TUC, but *anyone* concerned about the future of the country is a potential ally. I see in it the chance of enlisting the active support of many who have seen no connection between our present family allowances and their own particular interests. Politicians, employers and economists bothered about wage inflation should be allies. So should Common Market supporters; educationalists in many aspects; advocates of equal pay and of fair treatment for married women; those whose special interest is the deserted or unmarried mother; income-tax reformers concerned about incentives for the young family man; even those who complain that social security benefits are too lavish and are exploited by scroungers!

10 *Clawback*

TONY LYNES

Few Government measures in recent years have caused as much confusion and misunderstanding as the package deal by which, in 1968, the balance between family allowances and tax allowances for children was shifted in favour of the former. This reform, generally known as 'clawback', was basically simple and its effects easy to grasp once the underlying principle was understood. However, neither of the Government departments directly concerned (Inland Revenue and Social Security), made any serious attempt to explain what was being done, either at the time or subsequently. This note is intended to provide such an explanation, to show how clawback grew out of other proposals of a somewhat different nature, and to assess the relevance of this device as an anti-poverty measure for the immediate future.

Tax allowances as a subsidy

The idea that tax allowances can be regarded as a kind of subsidy, with effects that are in some ways similar to those of direct cash grants in the social security system, has a long history. Indeed, it was one of the arguments advanced by some advocates of family allowances during the long campaign which preceded their introduction in Britain in 1946. J. M. Keynes, for example, in 1940 described as 'highly anomalous' a system of tax allowances which, for a man earning £250 per annum, were worth £7 for the first child and nothing for subsequent children, while their value rose with income to a maximum of £18.75 for every child. He proposed that tax allowances for children should be abolished. In their place, a flat payment of £0.25 per week should be made for every child, regardless of the size of the parents' income.[226]

The reason why the value of tax allowances for children rises with income is that these allowances take the form of a deduction from the taxable income of the parents (in 1971-72, ignoring clawback, the deduction is £155 for a child under 11, £180 for those aged 11-15, and £205 for those of 16 and over undergoing full-time education). The value of the allowance for a particular child thus depends on the rate at which tax would otherwise have been payable on the slice of income in question. In 1968, the rates at which income tax (excluding surtax) was payable varied from nil to $41\frac{1}{4}$ per cent, with two intermediate stages (since abolished) of 20 and 30 per cent. A family with one child under 11, before the introduction of clawback, would have had its taxable income reduced by £115 (the allowance, at that time, for a child under 11). If the father was earning, say, £30 a week, he would have had to pay tax on that £115 at the standard rate of $41\frac{1}{4}$ per cent, but for the allowance. The value of the allowance at this level of income was therefore 115 times £0.41$\frac{1}{4}$, or £47.44. If the family's income had been lower, the allowance might have been worth less. For example, if the father's taxable income, after deducting any allowances to which he was entitled other than the child allowance, had been £300 or less, he would not have been liable to tax at the standard rate but only at the reduced rates of 20 and 30 per cent – or, if his income was very low indeed, he might have been below the income-tax-paying level altogether. In this extreme case, the effects of the child allowance would be to exempt from income tax £115 of income which would have been exempt anyway. To a man who is already below the tax-paying level, additional tax allowances are worth nothing.

As a method of subsidising families with children, therefore, tax allowances for children seem remarkably inefficient, since they are worth most to those least in need of such a subsidy, while the poorest families derive little or no benefit from them. Family allowances, on the other hand, are payable at the same rates to rich and poor alike. In some countries, they are not subject to income tax. In others, of which Britain is one, they are taxed so that only families with very low incomes get the full benefit of them, their net value falling by stages as the family's income rises. It is understandable, therefore, that those concerned with the abolition of poverty, rather than with equity as between families further up the income scale, should regard family allowances as a more sensible way of redistributing income in favour of families with children than tax allowances.

Tax allowances and equity

Equity in the tax system, however, is also a desirable aim. If a given amount of revenue has to be raised through the tax system, it is not unreasonable that a taxpayer with a wife and children to feed, clothe and shelter should make a smaller contribution to the total than a single man or woman or a childless couple with the same income. Indeed, if the object of tax allowances is to equalise the relative tax burden as between one taxpayer and another, one could argue not only that the allowances for children were too small but that their value should have been related even more directly to the family's income.

The suggestion that tax allowances for children should be reduced or abolished is therefore, at first sight, unattractive. As a way of paying for, say, better roads or subsidies to farmers, it would be indefensible, since the whole of the increased tax burden would fall on families with children. It is defensible only if the corresponding increase in government expenditure is devoted to an object so desirable as to outweigh the inequitable effect on the tax structure. And even then the taxpayer with children could fairly ask why the cost of this admittedly desirable object should fall on him. Why should the single and childless not pay their share?

CPAG's first thoughts

Arguments of this kind did not at first play much part in the deliberations of the Child Poverty Action Group, the outcome of which was the December 1965 memorandum to the Prime Minister,[227] which Frank Field describes in Chapter 12. He discusses CPAG's interest, at that stage, in an alternative to abolishing tax allowances as a way of paying for increased family allowances: the benefit of tax allowances could be extended, in the form of a direct payment, to those below the taxpaying level. Subsequent closer examination of this and other 'negative income tax' proposals showed, however, that this was not only an administratively questionable approach; but, as David Barker demonstrates in Chapter 5, it would have provided an inadequate remedy to family poverty. To have made the scheme more adequate by increasing the tax allowances would have had the expensive result of giving more to the rich as well as to the poor.

The Group's other proposal was both more adequate and more practical. Abolition of the tax allowances for children would have yielded sufficient revenue to meet most of the cost of increasing family allowances to the levels advocated by the memorandum: £0.50 a week for the first child, £1.25 for other children under 16, and £1.75 for older children in full-time education, all free of tax (in considering the implications of these figures, it should be borne in mind that family allowances were then £0.40 for the second child and £0.50 each for subsequent children, less income tax, and that average earnings were more than 30 per cent higher in 1970 than at the end of 1965). It was suggested that the part of the cost that was not covered by the abolition of tax allowances could be met by a system of contributions of which the single and childless would pay their share.

From the point of view of the low-income families it was designed to help, the proposal had obvious attractions. Most of those with incomes below the National Assistance scale would at least be raised above this modest level; and the increase in their incomes would not depend on their undergoing a means test or complying with complicated administrative provisions. For the better-off, its attractions were less obvious. Granted that single people and childless couples were to contribute to the cost, it remained true that, to a large extent, the proposal represented a redistribution of income from the not-very-rich to the poor *among families with children*. It thus invited the criticism mentioned above, that the cost of alleviating family poverty was to fall disproportionately on other families with children. This would have been a difficult policy to defend even if higher family

I

allowances had been universally regarded as a desirable object-ive. Given the widespread prejudice on this subject (a pecu-liarly British phenomenon), the political objections to the Group's proposal were formidable.

These objections were voiced in a number of quarters, usually in a tone of moral indignation from which one might have thought that the proposal was to transfer income from poor to better-off families, rather than the other way round. Among the more damaging attacks was that of C. N. Aydon, whose proposal to give families the option of family allowances (at an increased rate) *or* tax allowances was published in *New Society* in January 1967.[228] Aydon argued, inaccurately as he subsequently admit-ted, that under the CPAG proposals, 'the entire cost of substan-tially increased allowances for the poorer families would be financed, at a time of high taxation, entirely by sacrifices on the part of the better-off families with children'. Yet, while con-demning CPAG for wishing to deprive higher-income families of their tax allowances and to compensate them only partially by higher family allowances, Aydon apparently saw nothing wrong in his own proposal under which the same families would have had their family allowances confiscated with no compen-sation whatsoever!

CPAG's new approach: the clawback proposal

By the beginning of 1967, it was clear that a more sophisticated approach was needed if the reform of family allowances and tax allowances for children was to gain political acceptance. It was at this stage that the device now known by the rather repulsive title of 'clawback' replaced the cruder proposals described above. It was explained in a second memorandum issued by the Child Poverty Action Group in February 1967.[229] Whereas previously the reduction or abolition of tax allowances for children had been seen as a way of raising money which could then be spent on higher family allowances, clawback was *not* a way of raising money but rather a way of confining increased expenditure on family allowances to relatively low-income families. There was no longer any question of taking allowances away from the better-off to redistribute them to the poor. Instead, the better-off were to keep their existing allowances, though in future, if the Group's proposals were fully implemented, they would receive the whole amount as a direct cash payment instead of part of it taking the form of a reduction of income tax. Poorer families would benefit from the change, just as they would have under the original proposals, the cost of this additional benefit being borne by the Exchequer out of general tax revenue rather than by a specific increase in the tax liability of those with children.

The way in which this was to be achieved was so simple that it now seems incredible that it was not invented sooner. The Group proposed the following increases in family allowances:

Age of child	First child	Each subsequent child
	£	£
Under 11	0.90	1.22½
11 – 16	1.10	1.42½
Over 16	1.30	1.62½

These increases were to be paid tax-free to all families, regardless of their income from other sources. At the same time, tax allowances for children were to be abolished. The net effect, for a standard-rate tax-payer with one child under 11, would have been:

	Per annum
	£
Gain: Tax-free family allowance @ £0.90 per week	46.80
Loss: Abolition of tax allowance: £115 @ £0.41¼	47.44

For larger families or older children, the effect would have been the same: a family paying tax at the standard rate would have derived no net benefit from the increase in family allowances, since the additional tax payable would have balanced more or less exactly the additional allowance. In other words, the whole increase would have been 'clawed back'.

What made this approach feasible was the fact that the U.K. income tax system, though generally thought to be highly progressive (i.e. the higher your income the higher the rate of tax you pay), in fact taxes earned income over a very wide range at a single rate – the so-called standard rate, which was then

41¼ per cent.* (For a family of three, in 1967-68, this range was from around the average wage to roughly £5,000 a year). Since the value of a tax allowance depends on the marginal tax rate (i.e. the tax paid on the next £1 of taxable income), a given reduction in tax allowances will have the same effect, in terms of additional tax payable, on all standard rate tax-payers except those with incomes above or close to the level at which surtax begins. It was thus possible to use clawback to limit the benefit of an increase in family allowances to those with below-average incomes, without leaving the vast majority of families above this level either better or worse off by the exchange of tax allowance for family allowance. Part of the net cost might of course fall on such families, as on any other tax-payer, but there was no question of better-off families with children being deliberately made to bear an unfair share of the burden.

As surtax begins to operate at higher levels of income, the tax system again becomes progressive. Since the levels of family allowance proposed by CPAG were calculated to enable the standard-rate tax-payer to break even, surtax-payers with children would have been slightly worse off as a result of clawback. Curiously enough, this genuine unfairness, which is perpetuated in the Government's scheme, passed almost without comment, while opposition to clawback continued to focus on the supposed unfairness to the majority of tax-payers with children.

The Government adopts clawback

The Government adopted clawback, though the increase in family allowances fell far short of that demanded by CPAG:

	Before Oct. 1967 £	From Oct. 1967 £	From Apr. 1968 £	From Oct. 1968 £
Second child	0.40	0.40	0.75	0.90
Third child	0.50	0.50	0.85	1.00
Fourth and subsequent children	0.50	0.75	0.85	1.00

* The *effective* standard rate of tax on earned income was not 41¼% but 32%. Tax allowances for children (and other personal allowances), however, are deducted *after* calculating earned income relief, so that each £1 of allowances was worth £0.41¼ to the standard rate tax-payer.

Unlike the CPAG proposal, the Government's scheme entailed the continued taxation of family allowances, so that it was not the £0.50 per child increase that was 'clawed back', but the £0.34 that remained of that increase after tax had been paid at the standard rate. This was achieved by reducing tax allowances by £42 a year in respect of each child qualifying for family allowances. The effect, for the standard-rate tax-payer, was as follows :

	Per Annum £
Increase in family allowance (per child) @ £0.50 per week	26.00
Less tax @ 41¼ % on 7/9 of £26	8.34
Net value of increase	17.66
Reduction of tax allowances (per child) = 42 x £0.41¼	17.32½

A practical problem which had to be solved was the fact that many children qualify for tax allowance but not for family allowance : not only the first child in the family but children over 19, certain recent immigrants, and others. A general reduction in tax allowances for children would thus have hit a large number of families who would not derive corresponding benefit from the increase in family allowances. To get over this difficulty, instead of the tax allowance for *children* being reduced, the taxpayer's *total* personal tax allowances were reduced by £42 for each child qualifying for family allowance.

Had the whole operation been planned in advance, including the £0.15 family allowance increase to compensate for post-devaluation price rises, its effects would have been more easily understood. From the beginning of the tax year in April 1968, mothers would have received an extra £0.50 a week in family allowances for each eligible child. Fathers would simultaneously have had all or part of this increase deducted from their take-home pay, as a result of the adjustment of their tax allowances. What actually happened was more complicated, since the changes occurred, by stages, over a period of 18 months :

October 1967: Large families receive a first instalment of the promised increase in family allowances – an extra £0.25 a week for each child from the fourth on. No adjustment of tax allowances is made, since they cannot easily be reduced in the middle of the tax year.

April 1968: The remainder of the family allowance increase of £0.35 per child takes effect. This means that an extra £0.35 is paid for the second and third children in a family, but the increase for fourth and subsequent children is only £0.10. At the same time, tax allowances are cut by £36 per family allowance child, to clawback both the £0.35 increase and the further increase of £0.15 per child promised for October 1968.

October 1968: The £0.15 increase comes into effect. Since the corresponding tax adjustment took place in April, the standard rate tax-payer goes on paying the same weekly amounts of tax as he paid in the first half of the tax year.

April 1969: In the new tax year, the reduction of personal tax allowances goes up from £36 per family allowance child to £42 since the £0.15 increase, which was paid for only half the previous year, will now operate for the whole year.

The effect on standard rate tax-payers of the clawback operation was distorted in three ways in April 1968, and was further confused a year later:

April 1968

(*a*) Those with four or more children not only have to pay back the £0.10 increase for their fourth and subsequent children, but find that, in future, they will also have to repay the £0.25 that they have been drawing, without clawback, for the past six months. In the tax year commencing April 1968, therefore, their income tax goes up by more than their family allowances.

(*b*) Although the £0.15 increase is not to take effect until October 1968, the corresponding tax increase operates from the beginning of the tax year, adding $7\frac{1}{2}$p a week to the father's tax liability throughout the year in order to clawback £0.15 he will receive for only the second half of the year. In other words, he pays an extra £0.42$\frac{1}{2}$ tax each week throughout the year, against an increased family allowance of £0.35 for the first six months, and £0.50 for the second six months. This means an 'excess' payment in tax, from April to September 1968, of $7\frac{1}{2}$p a week, but a family allowance 'profit' of $7\frac{1}{2}$p a week from October 1968 to March 1969.

(*c*) Some weeks elapse before the reduction in tax allowances takes effect, since revised PAYE tables have to be distributed to employers. Consequently, several weeks' family allowance increase is clawed back from a single week's pay.

April 1969: It is only at this point that the standard-rate tax-payer begins to repay the full £0.50 increase, rather than £0.42½ a week.

Even without these multiple adjustments, some misunderstanding of clawback might have been expected, since it is not easy for tax-payers to disentangle the effects of the various factors which may cause their PAYE deductions to fluctuate from week to week. The piecemeal way in which the changes occurred ensured, in Moynihan's memorable phrase, 'maximum feasible misunderstanding'.

Spreading the confusion

Some of the misunderstanding came from surprising quarters. For instance, both the Prime Minister and the Chancellor of the Exchequer seem at first to have viewed clawback not merely as a way of *increasing* benefits on a selective basis by recovering the increases from the less needy recipients, but as a device for taking back benefits already in payment. Mr Wilson, announcing the decision to apply clawback to the £0.35 increase in family allowances, informed the House of Commons that the Chancellor was 'examining the possibility at a later stage of extending this principle of selectivity based on tax adjustments more generally through the family allowance system, not just the [£0.35] increase',[230] while the Chancellor himself expressed the hope that the following year he would be able to use this 'civilised and acceptable' form of selectivity to recover family allowances in full from those not in real need of them.[231] The implication of this threat, if it was to be taken seriously, was that tax allowances would be further reduced without any corresponding increase in family allowances; a totally indefensible way of selectively taxing parents!

Another source of misunderstanding arises from the failure to distinguish between the initial effects of clawback and its longer-term implications. The use of the term 'selectivity' in this context is misleading. It is true that the net benefit of the operation accrues only to low-income families. In this sense, it can correctly be described as a method of 'selectively' increasing the total value of allowances for children. Once the operation has been carried out, however, one is left with a more generous *universal* family allowance on the one hand and a tax system which takes less account of family commitments on the other. This is hardly 'selectivity' in the sense in which the term is normally used and which is adopted in Chapter 4 and the Conclusion.

One consequence of this fundamental difference between the immediate and long-term impact of clawback is that however ham-fisted the Government may be in introducing the changes in family allowances and tax allowances, any resentment that may be aroused soon fades as people get used to the new situation. Thus, the adverse reaction to the 1967-69 changes is already largely forgotten. As early as May 1969, Mr Crossman was able to welcome the 'on the whole friendly and understanding attitude . . . when people got used to it'.[232] Even more significant was the acceptance by Conservative spokesmen of the 'clawback' principle only two years after they had condemned its adoption by the Labour Government.[233]

Is there a future for clawback?

Despite Mr Iain Macleod's dramatic change of heart on the subject before the 1970 election, however, the Conservative Government has chosen to move in a very different direction in an attempt to tackle the problem of family poverty. Instead of higher family allowances, with or without clawback, there is to be yet another means-tested benefit – the Family Income Supplement. Whether the Government can fairly be accused of going back on its election pledges is a question on which opinions differ. What is certainly true is that clawback was in some respects a less attractive policy in 1970 than when the Labour Government decided to adopt it three years earlier. And the reasons why its attractions were diminished had little if anything to do with party differences.

One of those reasons is the abolition of the 20% and 30% rates of income tax by the Labour Government in its two budgets of 1969 and 1970. Ironically, it was partly the effects of the 1968 clawback operation that led to these changes in the tax structure. One of the less desirable results of the reduction of tax allowances in that year was to bring within the scope of income tax a large number of workers who were previously exempt because of the size of their families. This, however, was only one factor which had led to more and more low-paid workers being subjected to income tax. The failure of tax allowances in general to increase in step with wages over the years had meant a steady lowering, in relative terms, of the tax threshold. Income tax, once an essentially middle-class levy, had gradually infiltrated into the average manual worker's wage packet and even aggravated the poverty of some families with incomes below the supplementary benefit level.[234] There was clearly a case for raising the tax threshold, and the Chancellor of the Exchequer, Roy Jenkins, accorded higher priority to this objective than to a further instalment of clawback, which would have brought still more low-income families into the income tax net. He may even have believed, mistakenly, that raising the threshold would pave the way (to mix a metaphor) for the next clawback operation. This might indeed have been true if he had chosen the conventional method of raising the threshold – a straightforward increase in the personal allowances. Such an increase, however, would not only have had the effect of exempting from tax those just above the tax-paying threshold; it would also have reduced the tax liability of *all* tax-payers by exempting an additional slice of their income. To avoid giving this unwarranted and costly bonus to the better-off taxpayer, Mr Jenkins deprived him of the benefit of the increased personal allowances by eliminating the lower rates of tax:

Personal allowance :	*1968-69*	*1969-70*	*1970-71*
Single	£220	£225	£325
Married	£340	£375	£465
Tax rates :	£100 @ 20 %	£265 @ 30 %	All @ 41¼ %
	£200 @ 30 %	Remainder	
	Remainder @ 41¼%	@ 41¼%	

Taxpayers already paying at the standard rate in 1968-69 on part of their income found that the increased rates of tax payable on the first £300 of their taxable income in 1969-70 almost exactly balanced the increase in their personal allowances. For single people and working wives this was equally true in the following year. Married men, however, were allowed to make a profit of about £7 in 1970-71, since their personal allowance was raised by £90, while the single person's allowance went up by only £70. In both years, those previously paying tax only at the reduced rates gained from the combined effect of the changes, and many of them were exempted altogether. A neat application, one might say, of the clawback principle.

In effect, what Mr Jenkins had done to the standard rate tax-payer in those years was to increase the amount of his income that escaped tax entirely but to tax the whole of his remaining income at the standard rate. The standard rate of tax was thus payable at a considerably lower level of income in 1970-71 than in 1968-69. Just how much lower can be demonstrated by taking as an example a married man with two children under 11. In 1968-69, his tax threshold was as low as £644 (excluding family allowances), but he did not pay tax at the standard rate unless he earned £1,029 or more. In 1970-71, his tax threshold was £792 (again excluding family allowances), but at that level of earnings he at once began paying at the standard rate. The implications of these figures for any proposal to extend clawback are clear. The object of clawback, as implemented in 1968, was to limit the effective benefit of an increase in family allowances to those below the standard rate threshold. That threshold had been lowered, for the married man, by £237, so that a man with two children earning only £16 a week would have had the whole of his family allowance increase taken back by the taxman if the 1968 exercise had been repeated in 1970-71. If one takes the comparison back to 1967-68, the figures are even more striking, since clawback itself had the effect of lowering the standard rate threshold for families with children, as Sir Keith Joseph pointed out in the debate on the second reading of the Family Income Supplements Bill:

A married couple with three children came into the standard rate of tax in 1967 when the household income was £23. By 1970, after those three Labour Budgets, a married couple with three children began to pay tax at the standard rate when earnings reached not £23 but [£16.05]. Moreover, this figure cannot be judged just as £7 below the 1967 level because inflation had debased the value of the £ in the intervening years. Thus, people who are in the category of family poverty are now bearing tax at the standard rate level.[235]

And he went on to demonstrate that, whereas the Labour Government had been able to give low-income families an extra £47 millions at a gross cost of £180 millions, a similar £0.50 increase in family allowances in 1970, at a gross cost of £187 millions, would have benefited the poor by only £6 millions (of the remaining £181 millions, £158 millions would have been paid back in income tax and £23 millions would have been offset by corresponding adjustments in national insurance and supplementary benefits).

Following the increases in tax allowances for children in 1971-72, these figures would need to be revised. The level of earnings at which the three child family in Sir Keith Joseph's example would start paying tax would be raised, by nearly £3, to £19 a week. Against this, however, must be set the increases in wage levels in 1970 and 1971, which reduced the number of families below any given tax threshold. The combined effects of these changes has probably not added greatly to the potential of clawback.

It does not follow that a further instalment of clawback is necessarily ruled out as one possible strategy for raising the incomes of poor families; indeed, the cheapness of the operation might be regarded, in some circles, as a positive advantage. There is, however, another difficulty. Until recently, advocates of clawback assumed that, once the principle was accepted, there was no good reason why its application should not be extended at least up to the point at which child tax allowances were in effect eliminated. To go further than that and reduce these allowances to a minus quantity (i.e. to impose a tax surcharge for each family allowance child), while theoretically possible, was never seriously suggested, since it would obviously be difficult to explain to a man with children why he had to pay more tax on his wages than other men earning the same wage but with smaller families. What was not realised was that this situation would arise before the point of total elimination of child tax allowances was reached.

The reason for this is that family allowances, though payable to the mother, are taken into account in the father's PAYE coding, so that the tax deducted from his wages each week includes tax on his wife's family allowances. Most fathers are unaware of this fact, because the tax relief conferred on them by the child tax allowance outweighs the tax payable on the family allowance. An additional child thus reduces the father's net tax liability, despite the addition of the family allowance to his taxable income. If family allowances are increased and the increases are treated as taxable income of the father, then, unless tax allowances for children also rise, a point will eventually be reached at which tax on the family allowance for a particular child will exceed the value of the tax allowance for that child. Each additional child in the family will then increase the father's tax liability. If the increases in family allowances are matched by corresponding reductions in tax allowances (i.e. clawback), this point will be reached sooner. Thus it may be argued, para-doxically, that clawback actually reduces rather than increases the scope for further increases in family allowances – though this argument is only valid if future family allowance increases are taxable (exemption of a given amount of family allowance from income tax has precisely the same effect as a tax allow-ance of the same amount).

The implications, for the new Conservative government in 1970, of this second difficulty can be demonstrated by calculat-ing the net tax advantage of having a third or subsequent child, at 1970-71 tax rates (the figures would be slightly different for the second child, whose family allowance is £0.10 lower). Tax at the standard rate on the £1 family allowance, allowing for earned income relief, came to £0.32. The tax allowance for a child under 11 was £115, but this was reduced in effect by £42 as a result of the 1968 clawback, leaving £73, worth about £0.58 a week at the standard rate of tax. So the net tax advant-age of a third or subsequent child under 11 was £0.58 less £0.32, or £0.26 a week in 1970-71. This was very different from the pre-1968 situation. Tax on the £0.50 family allowance, at the standard rate, was then £0.16, while the tax allowance of £115 was worth £0.91, leaving a net tax advantage of £0.75. Increasing the family allowance by £0.50 in 1968, with claw-back, had the effect of reducing the net tax advantage to the father by the full amount of £0.50. A similar increase of only £0.25 would have sufficed, in 1970-71, virtually to eliminate the tax advantage altogether. A slightly bigger increase would have been possible for the second child, since a father of two children had a net tax advantage over a man with only one child of £0.29 in 1970-71. In view of these figures, it is perhaps not surprising that the Chancellor decided to increase child tax allowances in 1971-72, rather than reduce them by a further instalment of clawback.

The situation regarding the first child in the family is rather different, since family allowances start from the second child. Thus the father enjoys the full benefit of the £155 tax allowance for the first child, worth £1.15½ a week in 1971-72. It would be possible, therefore, to introduce a family allowance of £1.15 for the first child, with clawback to prevent taxpayers from deriving any net benefit from it, and without the father of an only child paying more tax than a married man with no children. Or one could arrive at virtually the same result by abolishing the tax allowance for the first child and making the proposed £1.15 family allowance tax-free.

Just how serious would be the objections to increasing the tax liability of fathers as their families increase in size, it is difficult to say. If the combined effects of family allowances and income tax were properly explained, most fathers would probably accept the situation as reasonable, given that the extra tax they would have to pay in respect of each child would be outweighed by the family allowances paid to their wives. Moreover, as the events of 1968 showed, the precise effects of changes in the tax structure are in practice obscured by income fluctuations, delays in printing tax tables, and other contingencies. Nevertheless, in view of the relatively small net gain to be obtained for low-income families from further family allowance increases accompanied by clawback, it seems clear that this device, by itself, no longer constitutes an adequate strategy for the abolition of family poverty in Britain, and still less for a more general policy of support for families with children, though it could well remain one important element in such a strategy.

11 *The potential and limitations of community action* *

RICHARD SILBURN

Until recently, such limited public discussion as there was about poverty was primarily concerned with what was normally thought of as a residual social welfare problem. Increasingly, however, as we learn more about such impoverished communities as St Ann's in Nottingham,[236] (and such communities will be found in every major town and city), poverty is seen to be infinitely more complex than this. Indeed, some traditional social work attitudes are seen to be positively harmful to the poor, as it becomes clear that poverty is not confined to a small group of problem families, but is widespread throughout many working-class communities. It is widespread, moreover, among people who do not require casework therapy, whose capacity for meaningful relationships will not be significantly improved by the ministrations of a social worker, and who have no need for advice about household management and domestic budgeting. Quite simply, the poor require more money, and given more money are perfectly capable of continuing to function independently.

But those poor who are condemned to life in one of our urban slums have additional burdens to bear. Poor housing is one such burden, and although the two problems of housing and material

* The present essay draws heavily on Chapter 11 of Coates and Silburn's *Poverty: the Forgotten Englishmen*. The author wishes to stress the considerable contribution of Ken Coates at every stage in the formulation of this general argument.

hardship can be bureaucratically distinguished, in real life they are often interlocked with one another so intimately as to become in practice inseparable. More than this, they feed off one another, because shortage of money can make substandard housing virtually uninhabitable, while the continued inconvenience of bad housing highlights and continuously emphasises one's impoverishment. Again, slum areas suffer from generations of public and social neglect, a neglect which meshes in with the 'private' distress caused by housing and money worries, and reinforces a sense of despair as a way of life, of hopelessness as the normal condition, a fatalism and a profound and permanent sense of insecurity which afflicts those who hover around a poverty-line as much as, and maybe more than, those living constantly below such a line.

Now the problems of poverty, of housing, and of environment are all recognised by authority, but are usually recognised separately. Thus any official social policy is liable to be, at best, fragmentary and partial, and in certain instances can do as much harm as good. For example, a perfectly laudable desire to improve housing standards will, if it involves (as it usually will) substantial increases in the level of chargeable rents on the new properties, put yet another pressure upon family budgets already stretched to their limits; the poor family's living standards will then have to be further reduced to meet the new rent, or the demoralising search for cheaper (and probably overcrowded as well as substandard) accommodation will start again. Similarly, expenditure on primary school improvements in the aftermath of the Plowden Report,[237] although desirable in itself, poignantly highlights the shocking inadequacies of the overcrowded homes for whose children the improved schools are to cater.

But quite as unwittingly destructive of morale has been the inability of bureaucratic authority actively to involve in community planning and decision-making the very people whose lives are so vitally affected by those plans and decisions:

Ours is a society in which, in every field, one group of people makes decisions, exercises control, limits choices, while the great majority have to accept these decisions, submit to this control and act within the limits of these externally imposed choices. It happens in work and leisure, politics, and education, and nowhere is it more evident than in the field of housing.[238]

Colin Ward's poignant complaint epitomises the grievance which has helped to stimulate the rapidly growing interest and experiment in forms of direct and meaningful grass-roots participation in, and control over, the affairs of the community.

Although it is true that tenants' associations have existed for many years as one form of community association, and although after the Second World War there was a widespread (but short lived) revival of interest in the community centre movement, the great impetus, in this country, to the community action programmes of today has been the far more urgent, dramatic (and successful) confrontation with authority by the homeless families in a number of local authority hostels, and even more recently by the squatters.

As early as 1962, a Mrs Sheila Jones, of the Tenants' Association at an LCC Halfway house, was writing:

> To some of us it is beginning to be clear that if we want anything done we will have to do it ourselves. The LCC tries to keep these places as terrible as possible to prevent others taking advantage of the 'facilities' provided. An imaginative and selective breaking of the artificial LCC rules might be an effective method of protest. What would happen for instance if a group of families got together and decided to bring in their own furniture to replace the LCC stuff? Would the LCC wardens call the police in . . . against tenants whose only crime was that they had tried, at their own expense, to make living conditions more bearable for themselves and their children?[239]

The following year saw precisely such a confrontation at Islington's notorious Newington Lodge, and in 1966 there were further persistent disturbances at the Kent County Council's King Hill hostel. Here the point at issue was the right of husbands to remain with their wives and children, a right that was disputed by the authority, outside specific visiting hours. Both these campaigns resulted in some welcome improvements in the administration of the hostels, and strikingly demonstrated that persistent and concerted action, even by the (initially) most demoralised and apparently powerless groups, even against the most authoritarian and insensitive of administrators, could be highly successful.

More recently, community groups have established themselves in towns and cities all over the country, and it has become quite modish to talk of citizen participation. The need for participation has even impressed itself upon some of our more flexible and astute public bodies, and the publication of the Gulbenkian Report,[240] followed by the Skeffington Report,[241] has rapidly given the whole subject an unexpected patina of respectability. Indeed, community participation is hailed by some of its more enthusiastic spokesmen as the definitive answer to all our urban problems. Consequently, it is high time that some attention was paid to some of the limits of community action, and to the alternative strategies that must be canvassed for dealing with those problems that are not amenable to local, community-based solutions.

The case of St Ann's

The St Ann's district of Nottingham, now in the throes of total demolition and municipal reconstruction, was, until the recent arrival of the bulldozers, a typical late Victorian, city-centre slum :

> The front doors open straight off the pavement and lead straight into the parlour. Access to the back of the house is usually through a narrow arched entry leading to the back-yards which are made of black brick. Sometimes these back-yards are open, communal. Rather more frequently, each house has fenced off its own portion, although as often as not access to one person's back-door may be gained only by walking through the neighbours' yards. At the end of the yards are lined the lavatories, in brick-built, sometimes tottering, sheds. The backyard serves as a playground for the children, and a meeting place for the adults. Many of the streets are cobbled, treacherous in the rain. A few are still gas-lit. Today these streets are often dirty and litter strewn . . .
> At first sight, this, then is St Ann's: a large deteriorated district, geographically distinct, with a certain sense of identity;

K

perhaps it might be expected, even of community: it is an area threatened with comprehensive demolition and reconstruction which is bound to change its whole character . . . an area of manifest environmental and social deprivation in which general amenities are at the most rudimentary level; where the scarce trees stand as stunted hostages to rotting bricks and grey stones; where until recently there have been no play facilities for the children except the yards and streets, and where, during our investigation, a little boy was killed while playing on a derelict site . . . where the schools are old and decrepit; with dingy buildings and bleak factories and warehouses, functionally austere chapels, a host of second-hand shops stacked out with shabby, cast-off goods; overhung throughout the winter by a damp pall of smoke. Greater familiarity with the district prompts other judgments, more difficult to sustain by physical evidence: to those of us who have come to know it and to feel involved in its life, St Ann's is an area dominated by a certain hopelessness, in which the sense that things are inexorably running down weighs constantly on every decision, and inhibits many positive responses to make or mend. And yet its people have, somehow, shaped out of this unpromising environment a way of living full of wit and humanity.[242]

St Ann's is a community with a very high concentration of family poverty. The St Ann's Study Group demonstrated that no fewer than 36 per cent of the households were in poverty, and that half the children in the district came from impoverished households.[243]

Certainly, St Ann's did not lack social and public problems, any one of which might well seem appropriate as a focus point for some form of community programme. Indeed the fact that the whole area was scheduled for comprehensive redevelopment by the Corporation was in itself a 'communalising' experience; it meant that while extortionate rents were paid by some people, and while the general deterioration of the area was very generally resented, everybody in the district had a common set of problems in his relations with the local council. An examination of the origin and development of a community action programme in the area points up some of the possibilities but also some of the pitfalls that present themselves.

The birth of the St Ann's Tenants and Residents Association (SATRA) came after the announcement of the intended demolition. The inhabitants had already learned, often through a grapevine in which rumour flowed as freely as fact, that the area was about to be flattened. Almost everyone in St Ann's was torn between two suppositions : that their house would be knocked down next year, or sooner, a belief that was encouraged every time an official-looking stranger walked down the road; and that they would rot on another twenty years without being rehoused, an assumption that floated to the top whenever the public authorities made any statement about the progress which was imminently to be expected. Hope is somehow less rational than cynicism in St Ann's. And until the public clamour reached deafening pitch, communications between St Ann's residents and officialdom were perhaps as intimate as they might be expected to be between, say, Chairman Mao Tse Tung and Generalissimo Chiang Kai-shek. Each side has, for a long time, known of the other's existence, and, in a more or less calculated way, tried to predict the other's movements. But aside from an occasional long-range broadside, or a hasty spy flight, neither has sought or found any contact with his opponent which comes any closer than adjacent columns in a distant neutral newspaper. When the original phasing of the whole area into separate demolition zones was undertaken, hardly anyone in St Ann's understood it, and virtually nothing was done by the Corporation itself to ensure that it be understood. The result was that, when Ray Gosling called a public meeting on this issue, over five hundred people turned up, primarily in order to try to find out what might be expected to happen to their house or street, and SATRA was formed.

The subsequent development of SATRA was markedly influenced by the enthusiasm of some of its more active members for the so-called 'Deeplish Solution',[244] that is to say for improving and refurbishing old properties rather than engaging in wholesale demolition, which demolishes community sentiments and kinship ties as assuredly as it removes unsatisfactory houses. When SATRA preoccupied itself with the demand for improvement grants for houses, its natural appeal was first of all to owner-occupiers. While, of course, there is every reason to press for improvement grants to be made available, and over a very much shorter run than the fifteen years which is the general rule, it remains true that an owner-occupier can still much more easily avail himself of such a facility than can a tenant. So that if a campaign is to be mounted on such an issue, it must be accompanied by a whole series of other campaigns aimed at assisting tenants, if the community association is not to become unbalanced in its composition and unrepresentative of the population at large.

This happened to SATRA, in spite of the fact that a lot of valuable work was put in by Ray Gosling and his colleagues. An initial recruitment based on the main demand for improvement grants resulted in the local membership being formed from a narrow sector of the St Ann's community, and this in turn resulted in the new Association taking up more and more of its time with problems of less and less general import, such as the difficulties of small shopkeepers faced by redevelopment which would remove their locale. These are important problems, but need to be construed in a total context, which can only be provided by a community association which represents a genuine cross-section of the local people, and can voice all their most pressing needs. Absentee landlords *do* exist, even in St Ann's. Repairs *are* neglected, even in St Ann's. And in St Ann's, most people are tenants and customers, not owner-occupiers or shopkeepers.

With community groups like SATRA it would often seem to be the case that the relatively more articulate people, and those whose felt interests are most directly threatened, easily become dominating influences. In the case of St Ann's, the proposed reconstruction represented to the shopkeeper a loss of business, and to the owner-occupier a loss of property, so that both groups were strongly and directly motivated to protest, and vigorously at that. The larger group of tenants and customers, on the other hand, were markedly less hostile to the redevelopment plans as such, and in many cases were strongly in favour of the redevelopment proposals. Their viewpoint was not strongly, consistently or primarily expressed by SATRA.

To the extent that community action groups do not, in practice, remain open to the whole population of their area, creation of a multiplicity of sub-groups may be called for. Indeed, it would be naïve to suppose, even in a small community (leave alone a district as large as St Ann's) that there is ever a perfect harmony of interests, exactly balanced and reflected in a community group. There is more likely to be a conflict, or partial conflict, of interests which will disrupt and fragment any local group which claims to defend the interests of all. In St Ann's, for example, there was a very widespread hostility between those who had lived in the area a long time, and newcomers to the district. This hostility was particularly marked in the case of coloured people or newcomers from overseas. Again there was another level of antipathy felt by the 'respectable' working-class residents towards alleged 'problem-families', whose presence was blamed for an overall lowering of social and personal standards.

The resolution of local and area tensions of this kind is impossible without the establishment of overall policy objectives capable of unifying all slum-dwellers in the recognition of a common interest, which can only be determined in relation to the overall social obstacles to the realisation of that interest. Of course, tenants, owner-occupiers, and even small landlords, taken in abstraction from their immediate environment, could easily be seen to have a great deal of common ground, if against their interests were weighed the alternative concerns of say merchant bankers, or captains of industry. But the last two groups of men do not commonly walk in the St Ann's of this world, and the vicissitudes of the interest rates which determine so much of local authority housing policy are seen, not as actions, results of human agency, but almost as natural phenomena, like earthquakes, or rainstorms on Cup Final Day.

None the less, housing and housing problems are one major public issue about which some sort of community programme could form and work, although as the example of SATRA shows us, a *simpliste* analysis of an apparently homogeneous district can lead to unforeseen distortions of purpose.

Let us be equally clear that there are some problems, however, which, no matter how heavily they may weigh upon a community, are yet not of the community in a way which makes a local solution possible. Poverty, in most of its manifestations, is one such problem. That the poorer people can be found in greater concentrations in some districts rather than others, does not mean that the causes of the poverty lie in the districts themselves. To talk in terms of local solutions in this situation is both misleading and misguided; indeed, to encourage a search for local solutions could be positively harmful. That there is widespread material hardship in St Ann's cannot be denied, but there is no St Ann's solution to it and to suggest that there is may prevent the poor (in such an area) from developing a sense of communality with the poor of other districts, and other towns. Anything which encourages a parish-pump chauvinism with reference to the problems of poverty, is as irrelevant and counter-productive as the equation of commonwealth immigration has been with the housing problem.

The limitations of community action

The wider sense of communality necessary to confront the poverty problem cannot express itself through purely local groups like SATRA, groups which command a geographically discrete loyalty. The problems of poverty require a different type of association, which operates at a different level. One such association is the Claimants' Union. This is an association of those drawing Supplementary Benefit, and aims to so organise and represent its members that everyone should receive their full entitlement : appeals against allegedly wrong or prejudiced decisions can be undertaken. As a welcome example of self-help through collective action and solidarity, this group deserves our warmest support. At the same time, of course, we must remember that the Supplementary Benefits Commission is not responsible for causing poverty in modern society, and it would be misleading if the Claimants' Union detracted attention from the wider question of wage and income distribution, the real cause of poverty. Knowledge of Welfare Rights is, at present, regrettably necessary : a longer-term ambition should be to abolish such a necessity. Frank Field develops this argument in the next chapter.

Clearly, there is a need for many different sorts of association. One of the major problems will be the relationship between these associations. Among many of those people most deeply and successfully involved in community work, there is a considerable and profound mistrust of other forms of association. Not only is the local council execrated, but so are the radical or one-time radical political parties, the Trade Unions, and other associations of a functional, rather than local, colour. Very often the distaste for such associations arises out of many years' frustrating personal experience of the ways of these bodies, and very many people will feel a considerable twinge of sympathy for this reaction. To ignore such organisations is, however, not a fruitful strategy; whether one likes it or not, they not only exist, but are really the only ones which exist to deal with those problems with a national sweep and structural roots, rather than purely local incidence. That the established organisations fail miserably is all too plain. But unless this failure is the subject of insistent public reproach, both from outside and within them, the danger is that the overall policies which are necessary will never emerge as practical alternatives. Direct action on the many grievances of the deprived population is a crucial lever to the development of its self-respect and social understanding; but it is not a sufficient remedy for its problems, which need overall solutions such as can only be canvassed by nationally structured political and social organisations. Unless a serious effort is made to shake them up, it is unlikely that any basic change will take place. To assume that such bodies can be by-passed is blithely optimistic; to assume that they could remain impregnable to insistent campaigning on these issues seems crudely pessimistic.

Very often the feelings expressed by community workers reflect a fear of being absorbed or taken over by national bodies, and hence losing both their sensitivity to local conditions, and their flexibility of response. There is, in consequence, a resistance to alliances between the community action groups and the trade unions and relevant political bodies. Whether one encourages such alliances on the formal level or not is very much a local decision, but participation in the affairs of the larger associations by no means necessarily assumes such formal alignments. If a community group succeeds in arousing into social action people who have hitherto confined themselves to private solutions to their public problems, then many of those people, aware of shared interests which cut across local and geographical boundaries, might well express themselves through political organisations and Trade Unions as well. Indeed, in this way, the more moribund constituency parties and union branches might be not only revitalised, but transformed into bases for the re-education and regeneration of their parent bodies.

Of course, historically, the vehicle which could have linked the separate efforts of community groups, trade unions, local councillors and other bodies, to provide both local servicing and communications, and a framework for the elaboration of national policy and demands, has been the Labour Party. The present crisis for the poor is aggravated to the extreme by the fact that the Labour Party seems no longer able to play any of its major traditional roles. Possibly it can never be recaptured for its own original purposes. It remains true, however, to put the matter at its worst, that before such a vast organisation can disappear from the scene, to make way for something more effective, all the issues it is presently balking must be seriously presented within it. Sooner or later this is bound to begin to happen. It will be time, then, to judge whether the attempt must fail. In the meantime, while agitation must be escalated on all other possible fronts, it must also be brought to bear on this one.

Perhaps the earlier criticism of fragmented and piecemeal bureaucratic policy-making can be reworked to some profit. It is not that local and national policies have neither place nor value; it is not that grass-roots, participatory associations can do either everything or nothing, and certainly the traditional associations offer no panacea. But all the policies and strategies mentioned have an essential role, not as alternatives to one another, but as complements to one another, and for any policy to succeed, there must be a parallel success in all the others.

The commitment that is required is a whole-hearted and comprehensive one involving traditional social welfare measures, a properly conceived and heavily redistributive incomes-policy, a housing programme, and, equally crucial but only recently acknowledged, the active encouragement of community action programmes which reactivate grass-roots democratic and collective participation in all levels of decision-making.

12 *A pressure group for the poor*

FRANK FIELD

In the spring of 1970, during the build-up to the general election, a bizarre confrontation was taking place. In the press, on the air, and in the country's leading debating forums, the Secretary of State for Social Services, Mr Crossman, and his Minister of State, Mr Ennals, were to be found defending the government's anti-poverty strategy against the charges of the Child Poverty Action Group's chairman and director.[245]

Why should the government have taken so seriously this 'pressure group for the poor'? How had a group operating from two attic rooms managed to become, in Mr Ennals's own words, 'a perceptive and articulate pressure group [whose] views are taken seriously both by the Government and by the informed public'?[246]

These are among the issues raised in this essay which describes the development of CPAG; traces the emergence of its policy; speculates on possible reasons for its successes; wonders why it has not been more successful; and discusses the rethinking that seems necessary if the Group is to fight a more popular campaign.

One evening after dinner

In early 1965, the Social and Economic Affairs Committee of the Society of Friends arranged a series of meetings on that recurrent topic, 'current social problems'. March 13 was the turn of Brian Abel-Smith who talked on 'a number of aspects of poverty'. The few people present were so stimulated that they arranged a follow-up meeting 'to consider what action ought to be taken to increase public awareness of poverty and to draw up a programme of action which would prevent and relieve it'.

One month later, the group reassembled as the *Advisory Council for the Alleviation of Poverty*. Its first action showed an immediate agreement on the political style the Child Poverty Action Group was later to follow : a memorandum was drawn up and presented to the Government. By lobbying the Minister responsible, the group made it plain that one of its tasks was to influence policy. However, none of the founder members thought in terms of a long campaign; they assumed that after a year, or at the most two, they would have achieved their original purpose. Indeed the group was so convinced about this that a year elapsed before it opened a bank account and almost as long before it accepted covenanted subscriptions.

Reform by memorandum

The first discussion paper to come before the group was written by John Veit Wilson and from it CPAG's most distinct characteristic became apparent.

Although 'action' had not been added to its name, the group made clear its overriding concern with the alternative lines of government *action* that could increase immediately the income of the poor. Yet an increase in family allowances, which was later to become an integral part of the Group's policy, was only one of the alternatives advocated. After further consideration, and a paper by Tony Lynes, the members, now calling themselves the *Family Poverty Group*, made their submissions to Mr Houghton, Labour's first overseer of the social services.

The group did not make its public debut until nine months after the first meeting at Toynbee Hall. In late December 1965, a number of distinguished social science academics, with CPAG's chairman, Fred Philp, signed a joint letter to the Prime Minister urging him to take immediate action on behalf of the poor. Accompanying this letter was the Group's second memorandum.

The core of this paper was the Group's insistence that 'it is necessary to find a way to increase the income of the poorer families with dependent children, both when the head of the household is employed and unemployed'.[247] Further, as the

Group had outlined in the memorandum to Mr Houghton, its belief was that 'this can best be done by increasing family allowances or by making some modifications of the child tax allowance system that will benefit poor families'.

In suggesting the first alternative, the Group proposed the abolition of both child tax allowances and existing family allowances, replacing them with a tax-free payment of £0.50 per week for the first child, £0.25 for all subsequent children under 16 and £1.75 for older children undergoing full time education. The second alternative was a development of existing PAYE machinery so that families not fully claiming their tax allowance would receive a reverse income tax payment.

The intellectual backing for these two alternatives was not the only feature of the campaign to catch the public's interest. Just before disclosing to the press its second policy document, two of the Group's ablest academics published *The Poor and the Poorest*. They showed that, in 1960, one in seven of the population had been living on incomes of less than 140 per cent of the basic national assistance scale; and two out of five of them were living in households that were primarily dependent on earnings.[248] For many who have kept abreast of CPAG's developments since 1965, the Group's policy statement and the research by Townsend and Abel-Smith have become inseparable. But even though these two events brought poverty back into the centre of the current political debate, they did not evoke a positive response from the Government for another 18 months. Indeed, by the spring of 1967, the Government's review of social security had already lasted more than two years without apparent results. The group therefore issued its third memorandum.[249]

Since the group's meeting with the Prime Minister, in 1965, the Government had been forced to take a series of savage deflationary measures. In these circumstances, it was natural for the Group to address its message to the Chancellor of the Exchequer. It tried to answer how help could be given to low income families 'without placing an excessive burden on the Exchequer'.

Its solution was to develop further the first alternative it had put before the Prime Minister. If immediate help was to be given to poor families, the only action open to the Government was to increase family allowances. Specifically, the Group asked that they should not only be increased, but weighted according to age and the number of eligible children. The cost of the proposed reform was to be kept to a minimum by 'clawing back' the universal increase from parents claiming child tax allowances, in such a way that no standard rate income tax payer became worse off by the change.

The government reacted as before. The poor would have to wait until the mammoth review of social security had been completed, and wait they did until July 1967 when the report of the Government's own enquiry into the *Circumstances of Families* was published.[250] Three weeks later, the Minister with overall responsibility, now Mr Gordon Walker, introduced the long awaited Government reforms. Family allowances were to be increased by £0.35 per child but, at the same time, a 50 per cent rise in the price of school dinners and welfare milk was announced.[251] This was hardly an adequate outcome of the Government's three and a half years' formulation of an anti-poverty strategy. In a reply to an immediate question, Mr Gordon Walker was forced to admit that half of those families with incomes below the official poverty line would remain there. And for some families, those with one child and just above the qualifying income for free school meals, the Government's action made them economically worse off.

Although the Government had accepted the Group's recommendation to increase family allowances, it postponed a decision on minimising the cost by simultaneous adjustments to tax allowances. It needed another massive deflationary package deal, the appointment of a new Chancellor and the devaluation of the pound before this aspect of CPAG's proposals was accepted.

In January 1968, at the same time as announcing a further £0.15 increase in family allowances, the Government accepted the Group's clawback proposal. But this increase in family allowances, coming quickly on top of the last, was not the beginning of a regular review of family allowance payments. The adjustment was a small concession to the Prime Minister's pledge, on television, that the poor would be protected from the effects of devaluation.

With clawback accepted, but with only inadequate increases in family allowances granted, the Group's fourth memorandum made out the case for an immediate and substantial rise in benefits. The demand was for a two-stage policy commitment. The first was for family allowances to be raised to £1.75 per week for existing beneficiaries. The second stage was the extension of family allowances to the first child and the implementation of a minimum wage.[252]

Tactics

One of the Group's recruiting advertisements claimed that poor families have benefited by about £50 millions a year from its activities. The same advertisement went on to say that the Group employed four staff, of whom two were part-time. How is it that such a small organisation has managed to exert such apparent influence? CPAG's main strength has been the agreement of its members to campaign around one key issue. From early 1967, the executive committee decided that an increase in family allowances was the only immediate and effective way of relieving family poverty. This is not to say that the Group has not pursued other, and sometimes unanticipated, lines of action. It has been heavily involved, for instance, in welfare law and welfare benefits.

On the former front, the group was soon involved in a campaign to beat the wage-stop[253] and, at the height of the debates on its 1970 policy statement, was still finding time to release a new guide to the wage-stop.[254] Like its new guide to supplementary benefit appeal tribunals,[255] this was largely the product of the Group's welfare lawyer and legal committee, whose appointments could hardly have been anticipated in 1965.[256] Both the wage-stop campaign and the appeals work have relied heavily on another unanticipated development: the growth of branches, starting in 1967.

Branches have played a big part in the Group's welfare rights activities which have culminated in the publication of *A Guide to National Welfare Benefits*.[257] Through their surveys,[258] leafletting[259] and information stalls,[260] and other ventures, CPAG's branches have done much to draw attention to unclaimed welfare benefits and to help improve publicity for them. Yet, the branches have been very much aware that they 'must do more to get across the message that the supplementation of inadequate incomes, by a series of means-tested benefits, is no substitute for a guarantee of adequate incomes, as of right'.[261] In fact, these 'rights' activities have not only had the effect of helping individual families, but, by showing the ineffectiveness, unfairness and divisiveness of means tested benefits, have played an important part in the campaign for increased universal social provision.

The second contributory factor to success has been the ability of the Group to supply 'the best information'. At each crucial stage in the Labour Government's review of social security, the Group presented it with a closely argued programme of action backed with the active support of some of the most able academic social administrators.

Professor Mackenzie, noting that organised attempts to influence public opinion are still an important part of British politics, argues that such campaigns are not so much concerned to create public opinion as to create an opinion about public opinion.[262] There are two main avenues open to groups wishing to create such an opinion. The first is to get issues raised on the floor of the House of Commons. CPAG, like similar groups, has found little difficulty in getting friendly M.P.s to keep issues on the boil, either by tabling Parliamentary Questions or by staging adjournment debates. The second avenue is to gain press coverage. As Professor Mackenzie notes 'the daily press is still held to be the best arbiter of public opinion . . . if only because circulation figures are related in some way or other to public appreciation'.

By operating both these options, it is possible to create an impression of a ground-swell in favour of a particular reform. With civil servants groomed, and politicians forced, to be conciliatory and to move in line with public opinion, both tactics play an essential part in a reformist group's campaign.

Two other points need to be mentioned to complete some of the background to CPAG's success. The first is that throughout the first five years of the Group's life there was a government in office mandated to combat poverty, and the Group always presented a programme as though the Government took seriously its socialist commitment. The second is the support of the trade union movement which, since the Second World War, has played some part in the campaign for increases in family allowances.[263] Why, with such powerful allies, has the Group not met with much greater success? Specifically, why was it that reforms costing only £40 millions (the net cost of implementing the first stage of CPAG's January 1970 proposals)[264] have met with such resistance?

What went wrong?

Part of the answer lies in the public confusion following the 1967 and 1968 announcements on family allowance increases, and the Government's acceptance of the clawback proposal only after part of the first increase had been paid to families. For families with four or more children, £0.25 of the £0.35 increase for the fourth and subsequent children came into operation in October 1967. The total increase was planned for April 1968 and, in the Budget of that year, the Chancellor would consider 'the method or methods by which the necessary revenue could be raised'. Before the end of the year, however, the pound had been devalued, and in a statement on the devaluation deflationary package deal in January 1968, the Prime Minister announced a further £0.15 increase in family allowances.[265] At the same time, he committed the Government to simultaneous adjustments in tax allowances so that much of the 1967 and 1968 increases would be 'clawed back' from the better-off families. But some families had been drawing part of the increase since the previous October and those paying the standard rate of tax had their tax codes adjusted in such a way that from April until October they were losing more than the weekly family allowance increase.[266] As Tony Lynes has noted, trying to explain to irate tax payers in April 1968 what had happened was not easy, even if the explainer understood what had happened.[267]

In addition to the confusion surrounding the increase in family allowances, there was the question of timing. It took the government over three years to announce any increase, and while the review of social security was being undertaken, the Government was remarkably busy pursuing a restrictive wages policy. Consequently, the reforms to help poor families were made at a time when those at work felt particularly aggrieved by other Government actions which penalised their efforts to earn a decent wage.

With the benefit of hindsight, one might attribute to the Group two important failures at a crucial point in its efforts to raise family allowances: it did not lobby anywhere near hard enough for a campaign to explain what clawback was and why it was being brought into operation; nor did it convince the Government of the need for a massive educational campaign on the extent of family poverty, and the importance of increases in family allowances to any meaningful anti-poverty strategy. With the lack of a positive lead, the welfare hawks found it easy to drag the increased allowances into the ever-widening work-shy/scroungers debate.

The result was catastrophic. The previous political antipathy to family allowances was doubly reinforced. And had the Group been successful in getting family allowances raised in election year, it would have been because of the campaign on the Government's social record, rather than a conversion to the principles underlying family allowances.

Post-election blues

We now know that Harold Wilson decided the date of the June 1970 general election four years before he made public his intention to dissolve Parliament and go to the country. Although CPAG did not share this secret, it was able to produce its own election manifesto. This stated:

> Three-quarters of a million children live in families which are poor. Some of these families are relatively poorer than those in poverty five years ago. Many other families find it difficult to attain what most of us would regard as a reasonable standard of living. It is in hope of getting these families a fair deal that this manifesto is submitted to the leaders of the main political parties.[268]

The response of the political leaders varied. The Liberal Leader, Mr Thorpe, managed to send a printed postcard saying that he had received it. Between walkabouts, Mr Wilson was able to reply that the Labour record spoke for itself, while the Conservative Party referred us to its election manifesto. This had an ambiguous sentence which read: 'We will tackle the problem of family poverty and ensure that adequate family allowances

will go to those families that need them'.[269] The Group took
this up with Mr Heath and asked whether the Conservative
manifesto reinforced the pledge, which Mr Macleod had given
on a number of occasions, that universal family allowances
would be accompanied by simultaneous adjustments to tax
allowances. On 1 June 1970, Mr Heath replied as follows: 'We
accept that, as Mr Macleod said in his budget speech, the only
way of tackling family poverty in the short term is to increase
family allowances and operate the clawback principle'.[270]

The election result will be known even to the least political
reader. Since the election, some of the more political have asked,
and that's putting it politely, if now, with the benefit of being
able to see more fully the consequences of its actions, CPAG
was right to attack the Labour Government's record, and to
help unwittingly the Conservatives – if only marginally – to win
the 1970 election. Certainly, the Conservatives made generous,
and not always very accurate, use of the Group's material; but
that was the inevitable outcome of the Labour Government's
refusal to direct more resources to the poor, although there was
nothing inevitable about the initial refusal. Indeed, the linch
pin of CPAG's strategy was that the rigorous questioning of
Labour's poverty record would somehow lead to a shift in
resources towards the least well off: surely, no party would go
complacently into an election year when its central myth was
being so critically examined? But we over-estimated the extent
to which politicians (like everybody else) respond in a totally
rational manner and under-estimated the way a Party's programme becomes like an offspring: to be criticised in private
but defended in public.

To say, as some more generous critics have, that CPAG lost
the election for the Labour Government ignores the widespread
disillusionment expressed ever since the 1966 deflation. Moreover, the post mortem by the most authoritative psephologist
did not even mention Labour's social policy, let alone
CPAG, as an election issue.[271] But if CPAG unintentionally
played a role, however small, in Labour's defeat, then given
the move towards inequality upon which this Government has
embarked, the Group acted against the poor's short-term
interests. Although at the time it was difficult to say anything
good about the Labour government, that administration has

L

taken on an almost Christ-like appearance in comparison with
the present Government.

Soon after the election results were declared, the House of
Commons, including the Government, dispersed for the summer
recess. Newspapers seemed eager to print any news suggesting
total Government inactivity. Here, we were told, was a Government which had unexpectedly won the General Election and
had little idea of what to do with its new-found power. These
illusions were quickly dispersed when Parliament re-assembled.
The Government had indeed gone off for the summer vacation;
but before they left, civil servants had been given their instruct-
ions on Mr Heath's 'quiet and total revolution in the British
way of life'.[272]

The 'quiet revolution' strangely sedated the Government's
commitment to the poor. By the autumn of 1970, the Group
heard that the Government was thinking of introducing a special
means-tested family allowance for poor families. The reason for
the Government's change of heart was necessarily nebulous.
However, this did lead the Group to stress the need to extend
family allowances to the first child. *A Better Tomorrow for the
Poor* outlined a programme which CPAG hoped met the
Government's new-found objections to family allowances.[273]

On 27-28 October, with the mini-budget statement[274] and the
publication of the FIS Bill (see Chapter 6), the Group learned
that this was not so. The mini-budget made three major changes
in Government policy which have had, and will continue to
have, a profound effect on the living standards of poor people.
First, Mr Barber announced cuts in public expenditure. The
major cuts were very largely accounted for by increased social
service charges. Secondly, he announced a reform of the agricultural support system, and still six months later, we did not have
the details of these proposals. Likewise, we still awaited the 'nitty-
gritty' of Mr Walker's reform of council house subsidies. Although this is intended to combat poverty caused by high rents,
as well as eliminate 'unnecessary' subsidies,[275] there is little doubt
that the reform will be ineffective with regard to the former
aim, but remarkably successful in cutting down the amount of
money allotted to housing subsidies. With the Government's aim
of saving between £100m and £200m on housing subsidies
by 1974-75,[276] it will be impossible to devise a rebate system

generous enough to eliminate poverty caused by high rents.[277] To do this, the Government will need to increase the resources devoted to housing subsidies; not cut them.

By 1975-76, the Chancellor's aim is to cut public expenditure by £1,500m. With such demands being made upon the Exchequer, it was surprising – to say the least – that £7m could be found to finance the Family Income Supplement. Sir Keith Joseph told the House that this £7m (plus £1m for wage-stopped families and £600,000 in administration) would mean that more money would go to poor families than if his party had carried out its election pledge of spending £30m on increasing family allowances.[278] The reasoning behind this, which would have delighted the most humble medieval mystic, has been critically reviewed elsewhere.[279]

While the increased social service charges were to come into operation in April 1971, FIS was not to become operational for another five months. What was the Group to do, therefore, in its campaign to increase family allowances? Could one expect a Government, even one with limited respect for the facts, to increase family allowances and thereby make many families ineligible for income supplements – even before the FIS scheme came into effect?

Obviously not: the Group decided, therefore, that its annual visit to the Chancellor should be concerned not only with its perennial plea for an increase in family allowances, but with a demand to raise the tax threshold. For reasons explained in Chapter 10, this was an essential first step to making clawback a more effective 'civilised form of selectivity'. In its 1971 memorandum to the Chancellor of the Exchequer, *A Plan to Help Low Paid Workers and Overcome Family Poverty*,[280] the Group drew attention to the number of workers who do a full week's work, earning less than their theoretical supplementary benefit entitlement, but paying tax at the standard rate. The memorandum outlined two alternative ways of introducing a minimum earned-income relief which would lift out of tax workers earning poverty wages. Alas, our explanations must have been inadequate, for instead of opting the poor out of tax, the Chancellor effected our proposal to the higher reaches of the tax range, so that those at the top paid less tax.

Apart from these changes, the Budget redirected to taxpayers the enormous budget surplus. This redirection of funds, which commenced with Mr Jenkins's last budget, means that £1200m will be returned to tax payers by the end of the financial year. The sum going specifically to families totals £215m: £207m in child tax allowances, benefiting the by-and-large richer tax payers; and £8m-odd to the very poorest families. If this country had an effective family lobby, as some European countries have, would so little have been directed to our most important investment – children? Although in other spheres of social policy it has been shown that the middle class tend to benefit disproportionately, would the same apply to cash payments? If the answer is 'No', then more attention ought to be given to the possibilities of using the undoubted strength of a middle class lobby on behalf of the poor.

A family responsibility payment

Before a more popular campaign can be launched, however, certain major stumbling blocks need to be overcome.

In the first place, a new family benefit scheme must appear to be fair to everybody. The present system fails patently in this respect: half the families with children do not receive any family allowance (as they have only one dependent child);[281] and for those that do, payment starts after the birth of the second child when most families have already adjusted to the loss of the mother's income.

Secondly, the new allowance needs to be paid in such a way as to create an obvious incentive to work. Despite much of the current anti-scrounger debate, the present scheme, as Sir John Walley emphasises, already fulfils this requirement, since allowances are paid when the father is in work but are subtracted from supplementary allowances when he is unemployed. But because the payment is made to the mother, this aspect of it is lost. Consideration should be given to the possibility of paying the new benefit into the wage packets of working fathers. Special provision would have to be made, of course, for the self-employed, while those drawing national insurance and supplementary benefits would have their allowance paid as part of the scale rates.

Thirdly, the children's benefit received by the lowest paid

working man ought to be as large as that paid to a non-working father.

Finally, the new benefit scheme should entail a flat rate universal payment which is adjusted annually in the November review of supplementary benefits. And it is necessary for payments under any new scheme of family support to be large enough to form an important part of most families' budgets. In this way, even the articulate middle class would have a vested interest in a satisfactory annual review on behalf of all children, including poor children.

Conclusion

DAVID BULL

The essays in this book have demonstrated the failures of selectivity; the shortcomings of NIT and FIS; and the limitations of family planning, as solutions to family poverty. Advocates of such measures ignore, or misconceive, the *causes* of poverty. The essays on a minimum wage and family allowances, on the other hand, see poverty in a wider social and economic context and take account of the dignity of those who need help. A similar orientation is demanded from lobbies for, and of, the poor.

The failures of selectivity

Tony Lynes, Sheila Kay and David Collard have demonstrated the failure of selectivity to achieve its goals.

But what is this thing called 'selectivity'? Two leading experts appear to disagree. Townsend thinks in terms of

> a test of means or of income . . . applied to the population in general, or indeed even to a particular category of the population, like fatherless families, the blind and the disabled, to decide who is poor enough to be provided with cash benefits, or free services, to be excused charges or pay lower charges.[282]

Professor Titmuss, on the other hand, does not insist on a test of income when he talks of 'selective services provided, as social rights, on criteria of the *needs* of specific categories, groups and territorial areas and not dependent on *individual tests of means*.[283]

The difficulty arises because the two terms 'universal' and 'selective', when used literally, are not mutually exclusive. A benefit that is given to every member of a category may be termed 'universal'; yet the very process of determining the boundaries of that category could be called 'selectivity'. For instance, family allowances are generally thought of as universal; but, pursuing Titmuss's definition, they would be selective, in so far as they are restricted to second and subsequent children under school leaving age. Life is rather less complicated, therefore, if one uses Townsend's definition, as do Lynes (Chapter 10) and Collard.

By using 'selectivity' in this sense, the anti-selectivist makes it quite clear what he is objecting to : it is the practice of determining eligibility by an individual test of means. We shall see, later in this chapter, how the withholding of family allowances from first children has split the interests of families, but this practice is not divisive along socio-economic lines. It is the restriction of benefits to those who satisfy a means-test that results in the indignity and humiliation to which Tony Lynes and Sheila Kay object.

It would be a mistake, however, to assume that the consistent adoption of this, or any other, definition implies the taking of a firm position in one of the two camps. David Donnison has observed that 'any intelligent man must be sometimes "selectivist", sometimes "universalist" '.[284] He gives examples of how he, himself, has sometimes qualified for one, and sometimes for the other, of 'these tawdry epithets'. Similarly, Collard's overall case against selectivity is not undermined by his support for means tests in housing as 'expedients for making the best of a bad job : so long as we have such an inefficient system of housing subsidies and such an unfair form of local taxation, we must tolerate rent and rate rebates' (p. 41). And David Barker, for all his arguments against selectivity, welcomes the extension of rent rebates to the private sector as a way of achieving greater equity between private and municipal tenants.

This lends support to Donnison's argument that

there is no *central question on selectivity*. There are a lot of different and rather complex questions to which such simple slogans offer no useful guidance.

Donnison has little patience with those who so simplify and polarise the conflict between universality and selectivity that it becomes the 'most misleading of all trivial dichotomies'.[285]

Because of the complexity, because of over-simplification, and because definitions are so hard to find, it seemed desirable to pause, at this point, to look carefully at the way in which the case against selectivity is presented in this book. We find that selectivity is defined in Townsend's terms and that the writers on selectivity share a common objection to the social divisiveness of individual tests of income, although means tests may have to be tolerated for a while, in housing, on grounds of expediency or of greater equity between groups.

Sheila Kay's concern extends beyond the stigmatised individual to the 'socially stigmatised area', where 'you can't get a hire purchase agreement'; and sometimes 'you can't get a good job' either (pp. 34-5). The need to discriminate *positively*, in favour of those who live in such areas, is not developed in this book. A useful discussion of this policy can be found in a paper by Robert Pinker.[286] He distinguishes between the *exclusive* device of selectivity and the *inclusive* strategy of positive discrimination. While the latter is 'a process of diagnosis and selection free from stigmatisation in so far as it aims at raising standards to the best possible level rather than the minimum level tolerable', selectivity entails 'processes of exclusion', like stigma, complexity and secrecy.

It will be noticed that this distinction is consistent with Townsend's definition; according to Titmuss's criteria, on the other hand, positive discrimination is a form of selectivity. Again, the value of Pinker's distinction is that it concentrates on the deterrent effect of an individual test of means: 'the effect of stigma is to make the discrimination take a negative form. The most ruthless form of selectivity is the human psyche responding to shame and humiliation'.

Mrs Kay describes some of the responses that she and fellow members of CPAG's Merseyside branch have encountered. Her case-studies underline the important fact that the administration of means tests still inflicts shame and humiliation *today*;

one does not need to summon up stories of the 1930s. Lynes, too, is concerned that the dignity of the claimant is *still* affronted. Need he, for instance, tolerate, from officials, contempt or obsequiousness; and does he have to complete application forms 'under dire threats of prosecution for making a false declaration' (p. 20)? Lynes concludes that the pursuit of dignity is 'intimately linked' (p. 27) with the goal of efficiency. This obvious point has been overlooked too often by advocates of means tests. If just one eligible person is deterred, in any way, from claiming a selective benefit, then the method is not efficient.

The pretence that means tests are an efficient way of concentrating help on those who most need it cannot be maintained: they discriminate in favour of the most articulate, the least proud, and those who are in contact with the more helpful social service agencies. By using means tests to spare the taxpayer 'wasteful' expenditure, the costs of social benefits are switched to those who fail to claim their rights. 'It is disgraceful', Collard argues, 'that society should want to make those sections of society least able to afford it bear the costs of selectivity'. (p. 39).

It should be noted that this important argument, which is not a common feature of the universalists' case,[287] comes from an economist. For some selectivists seem to believe that universality is a foible of sociologists.[288] Professor Titmuss is found guilty of 'amateurishness in the deployment of economic terminology'.[289] His quoting of such economists as Arrow and Boulding in support of his 'commitment' cuts no ice with Arthur Seldon, the arch-selectivist, since '1200 economists in the USA . . . have jointly commended [selectivity] as a device to deal with the removal of poverty'. Such is the force, in America alone, of 'what may properly be called the liberal counter-revolution in economic thinking'.[290]

Like Arrow and Boulding, Collard has not been caught up in this counter-revolution. He questions the economic efficiency of selectivity, concludes that 'real resource costs will almost certainly be higher under a selective than under an alternative universal system' (p. 43) and thinks it odd that those counter-revolutionaries 'who claim to attach so much importance to what the country can "afford" in economic terms, should so easily confuse real resource costs with exchequer costs'. For they have omitted, from their equation, 'time and trouble' costs; and the administration of means-tests involves considerable hidden costs. Some of these have recently been charted: twelve times as many officials are needed to administer supplementary benefits for two and a half million claimants as are required to operate family allowances for more than four million families;[291] the cost of checking fraudulent claims is likely to be out of all proportion to the sum recouped;[292] while experiments, by CPAG[293] and the National Suggestions Centre,[294] have shown the prohibitive amount of home visiting and regular following-up that would need to be done if means-tests were to succeed in concentrating help where it is most needed.

NIT and FIS

As they have come to recognise the failure of means-tests to achieve this concentration, some selectivists have turned to a negative income tax as 'a system which automatically identifies need and which automatically, and quickly, concentrates help where that need exists'.[295]

David Barker questions this argument. To contend that NIT would be automatic, administratively simple, objective and not humiliating is merely to say that it would be an improvement on means-tests, while ignoring the alternative of universal allowances which would satisfy better these criteria. He discusses eleven other arguments that have been advanced in favour of NIT and concludes that only two of these are substantive: family allowances have failed to eliminate poverty; and NIT would concentrate help where it is most needed.

The first of these arguments, Barker asserts, does not lead us, logically, to the replacement of family allowances but to their improvement. The fallacy of the second argument is a central feature of his chapter. True, the proposals of an IEA Study Group would lift all poor families above the supplementary benefit level – provided that *real* housing expenditure could be included in the assessment; but the schemes of Lees and Hayhoe, which have been taken up by Conservative politicians,[296] would raise to these heights only 20 and 40 per cent of poor families, respectively, compared with the 49 per cent achieved by the £0.50 increase in family allowances during 1968. Of course, NIT schemes *could* be designed to raise more people above this level, but the saving in public expenditure would then be smaller. Barker reminds us often of this dilemma for those advocates of NIT who promise relief to the taxpayer. Moreover, any attempt to be generous also conflicts with the assumed need to maintain incentives to work.

Barker shows how ungenerous the leading NIT schemes would be as a result of their effort to avoid 'indiscriminate benefits' : a three-child family with an income exceeding £16.95 would not benefit from even the most generous of them. And these inadequate benefits would be achieved at the expense of those with incomes just above these limits, especially in those variations of NIT that would take away their family allowances.

This is an important point to emerge from this incisive analysis. We must not be misled into thinking that we are all agreed on the virtues of NIT and need merely to iron out administrative difficulties. When politicians of all shades are being won over by the advocates of NIT, then, as Barker points out, 'it probably means that someone, somewhere, is missing the point' (p. 51). Certainly, for those who seek a solution to poverty not in the raising to a certain level of a small minority but in a wider redistribution of income, 'NIT is a strategy to be viewed with considerable suspicion' (p. 66). Impracticability is a red herring; Chapter 5 is a timely demonstration of how and why 'ideology starts to loom rather larger than impracticability' (p. 68).

Barker's objections to FIS follow much the same pattern. There is, however, one major difference : the automatic, 100 per cent uptake that is claimed as NIT's main advantage does not obtain for FIS. Otherwise, Barker demonstrates that the case for FIS rests, like that for NIT, on the false assumption that other social reforms could not be effected in order to achieve, as well or better, the aims of this new scheme. And he concentrates on the same issues of generosity, incentives and the wider implications for the Government's social strategy.

The burden of Sir Keith Joseph's case for FIS was that family allowances would be a less effective alternative. That they could not provide sufficient help 'without going into astronomic figures' was only one of Sir Keith's objections to family allowances (p. 72); but Barker demonstrates that the other two arguments have also to be seen in the context of the government's aim to reduce public expenditure. More will be said below on the argument that changes in the tax threshold have limited the scope of clawback; suffice it to say, here, that Barker shows this to be not so much a *technical*, as a *political*, matter : if the government had wanted to increase and claw back family allowances, it could have lifted the tax threshold. And while he acknowledges that its help for the first child is something to be said for FIS, family allowances *could* have been reformed to this end; Barker argues that the difficulties involved in introducing the scheme quickly were probably a less important objection than was the cost.

FIS does not *have* to be a parsimonious solution : the Government *could* decide to raise the 'prescribed amount' or lift its upper ceiling. Barker demonstrates how the proposed scheme is particularly ungenerous to larger families and higher rent-payers. In view of the Chancellor's stated intention to reduce housing subsidies, the latter group may still find themselves in poverty when the new rent measures are introduced. Moreover, other features of rent regulation and administration suggest that Sir Keith Joseph is optimistic to assume that Mr Walker's new measures will safeguard the position of those who are not helped by FIS.

The combined effect of superimposing FIS and an extended rent rebate scheme on the present system of means-tested benefits will be to increase the marginal tax rate for these groups. As Barker points out, this is hardly consistent with the Government's policy for increasing incentives for the better-off; but he reminds us that there is no proved connection between marginal tax rates and incentives. So long as the Government assumes a connection, however, there is, as with NIT, a conflict between generosity and incentives.

Sir Keith Joseph has observed that unless we ignore the possibility of disincentives 'and fill 100 per cent of the gap between a household's income and the make-up level, then automatically we shall be failing to reach the so-called poverty line' (p. 82). Barker objects to the policy of tackling poverty by bringing up to a line as many people as the government says it can afford to help : 'the strategy implicit in FIS is precisely that for which NIT was criticised'. He concludes that 'ultimately, the debate between proponents of FIS (or NIT)-type solutions and most universalists is not over means (how an agreed objective is best achieved) but over ends (how much inequality we are prepared to tolerate)'.

Family planning

Audrey Smith arrives at a similar conclusion: although family planning may contribute to 'the *alleviation* of poverty . . . when we discuss the *causes* of poverty, we need to turn to the more fundamental issue of unequal distribution of wealth and earned income' (p. 92).

She is afraid that support for family planning, as part of an anti-poverty programme, might help to perpetuate the myth that high fertility is a major cause of family poverty. Larger families may be poorer; but most poor families are small.

Mrs Smith uses case-studies to illustrate a variety of attitudes that prevent the regular use of birth control. She distinguishes the *unconfident*, victims of apprehension, fear, embarrassment or distaste; the *ambivalent* who know they should not have more children, but who are delighted when they find another baby is on the way; the *antagonistic*, to whom 'God', 'Nature' and 'Fate' are synonymous and to blame; and the *child-preferring* mothers who just love children.

These case-studies leave no room for complacency that the increased use of family planning depends *simply* on better propaganda and education. There are other obstacles too. Not only is knowledge about family planning often communicated as inadequately as are the welfare rights described in Chapter 2; the subject is likely to be even more embarrassing for the supplicant. A clinic-based organisation, Mrs Smith argues, is bound to exacerbate the 'feelings of embarrassment, insecurity and suspicion' (p. 90). It says much for the Family Planning Association that it has so often overcome these difficulties; but it is a pity that its conferences should discuss family poverty 'with inadequate attention to its causes' (p. 92).

We have seen how advocates of selectivity, NIT and FIS also ignore these causes. John Hughes and Sir John Walley, on the other hand, set their proposals, for a minimum wage and family allowances, in a wider social and economic context.

A minimum wage

John Hughes reminds us constantly that a minimum wage is 'only one element in a complex economic strategy' (p. 101). He is not, for instance, deterred by arguments that a minimum wage would result in price increases: the impact could be lessened by higher agricultural subsidies; a reduction, or even the abolition, of SET in the food distributive trades; and a similarly selective policy, in these industries, for VAT. Selective reductions of SET might also play an important part in avoiding the feared increase in unemployment: the criteria for reductions might be the nature of the industry (especially food); the region; or the ages of the workers.

Although he regrets that wages councils 'have done so little . . . to level up the lowest paid trades' (p. 97), Hughes wonders whether 'a revamped system of wages councils' (p. 104) might provide a suitable basis for a statutory minimum wage. This might entail a regrouping into larger 'sectoral' councils, and the development of a central supervisory body which would offer expert services. The new councils would be responsible for achieving earnings and conditions compatible with those in unionised industries; encouraging the unionisation of their own industries; and making more efficient the utilisation of labour in their sectors.

Despite his offering a way to build upon the existing machinery and answering the common objections to a minimum wage, Hughes is unlikely to convince the more ardent opponents of this policy; and even neutral observers may reasonably demand solid research evidence before they accept that the twin bogeys of inflation and unemployment have been laid. While we await such evidence, it cannot be denied that John Hughes has presented a well-reasoned case for a minimum wage – provided that it is part of a wider strategy that tackles taxation, collective bargaining policy and economic management.

Family allowances

Moreover, since it cannot take account of family responsibilities, a minimum wage can only be a *complement* to, never an alternative, to family allowances. Sir John Walley reminds us that this was Pitt's objection, 175 years ago, to Whitbread's minimum wage bill. Pitt's alternative proposal of family allowances might have been realised, Sir John suggests, had his bill of 1796 not been, in some ways, more ambitious than the Beveridge Report of 1942. Sir John goes on to present a depressing account of lost opportunities in the struggle for family allowances. Unfortunately, when the struggle was won, family allowances were sold to the nation as part of a strategy for arresting the decline in the birthrate. Sir John wonders whether Churchill's use of this argument in 1943 'may have a lot to do with the widespread belief that family allowances promote births . . .' (p. 110). Certainly, this is one of the objections that CPAG speakers have encountered, but it has seldom been a major bone of contention. This is borne out by two recent surveys by the Group.[297] The main complaint, in both surveys, was that family allowances are not spent on children.

There was little sign of the objection that family allowances encourage idleness. Yet CPAG speakers continue to come across this belief, which must be the most easily refuted misconception about family allowances. However much we may quote the international statistics, we cannot *prove* that family allowances do not encourage large families. Nor may Family Expenditure Survey data convince some audiences that boozing, betting and smoking are not prerogatives of the poor.[298] Yet once people realise that family allowances are *additional* income for the low-paid workers, while they are *subtracted* from supplementary benefits, it is difficult for them to sustain a belief that these allowances are a disincentive to seek work. If only this could be got across, then the incentive argument would be 'the easiest way of presenting the case for family allowances in Britain' (p. 108) and the public might come to accept that 'the real beneficiaries of increased family allowances are responsible citizens in regular work; all that the shiftless and irresponsible get from them is a better incentive to be less shiftless and more responsible' (p. 111).

Frank Field believes that this message might be better understood if family allowances were paid to fathers, but this lets off lightly successive governments that have failed to sell post-war family allowances as something different from the original com-

modity that Churchill offered the nation in 1943. Of course,
a Labour government that claimed to have abolished destitution
and a Conservative regime under which people had 'never had
it so good' could not be expected to develop a convincing case
for family allowances. And there was clearly no connection
intended between the Conservative promises, of 1970, to increase
family allowances and to eliminate 'the shirkers and the scroungers'.[299] The latter vow meant that the Conservatives would
tighten Labour's anti-abuse screw of 1968,[300] and the announcement of a committee of enquiry[301] into abuse is the first step in
that direction. More might have been expected, however, of a
Labour government that launched an enquiry into the extent
of family poverty and, on publication of its findings, announced
the first increase in family allowances for twelve years. All that
seemed to happen, however, was that the Labour Government
was too scared by the unpublished findings of its 1968 survey of
public opinion on social security benefits to make any further
increase apart from its post-devaluation £0.15. For although
CPAG's two limited surveys have shown that some of the myths
about family allowances may not be so widespread as we may
have feared, there can be no doubting that family allowances
are an unpopular benefit. In a survey of mothers of dependent
children, in 1957, this was the only social service on which a
sizeable proportion (20 per cent) thought less should be spent.[302]
Ten years later, a *New Society*/Research Services survey revealed
that family allowances still stood out as the most popular choice
for a cut in expenditure.[303] In this survey, like those of the
IEA,[304] it was pensioners who commanded public sympathy.
Moreover, the view that 'parents should subsidise their own
children' was voiced more strongly by manual workers than by
non-manual workers.

Clawed back or tax-free allowances?

As if family allowances were not unpopular enough, the government managed to make matters worse by failing to explain its
clawback measures. Chapter 10 describes the stages by which
this method of concentrating, on the lower-paid, the increase in
family allowances, was introduced without any attempt at an
explanation. Frank Field is doing CPAG injustice by suggesting

that it should have lobbied harder for an official explanation of this new measure: the Labour Government failed in this respect, as two of its leading social security spokesmen admitted to the Group's Annual Conferences of 1969 and 1970.[305]

Some of us have felt, when speaking on behalf of CPAG to various organisations, that the resistance to clawback has lessened as it became better understood and as the short-term injustices, described in Chapter 10, were ironed out. Mr Crossman was coming to the same conclusion by mid-1969[306] and CPAG's survey of parliamentary candidates supported this view.[307] Yet although only a fifth of candidates had received complaints that clawback had resulted in an irksome tax increase, we have to recognise that when the cry of 'reduce taxation' is raised in opposition to that of 'improve services', clawback helps to contribute to the higher taxes side of the account. The fact that only the surtax payer is any worse off may be lost in this sort of equation; indeed, this may be another good reason for adopting Frank Field's suggestion of paying family allowances to fathers.

The case for such a change could become greater once further clawing back brought about the situation where fathers with children paid more tax than did men earning the same wage but with no children. Lynes explains, in Chapter 10, how this could happen. While this provides a convincing, theoretical argument for paying family allowances in the father's pay packet, it seems unlikely that today's parliament would look any more favourably on such a proposal than did their predecessors of 1945.[308]

Lynes does not contemplate such a drastic measure: he hopes that 'if the combined effects of family allowances and income tax were properly explained, most fathers would probably accept the situation as reasonable' (p. 133). But are the Government and the mass media capable of explaining this relationship? Lynes's own account of the confusion spread by the Prime Minister and the Chancellor of the Exchequer is hardly encouraging.

Even supposing that clawback became fully understood and acceptable, there is, however, another important shortcoming. Changes, in 1969 and 1970, in the tax threshold have resulted in the situation, which Lynes explains, where a father of two children, earning £16 a week in 1970-71, would have had clawed back the full increase if the 1968 exercise had been

M

repeated. It should be noted that this is only one potential feature of a bizarre situation, which has been exposed recently by David Piachaud, where 'the current tax threshold is lower than the level of living provided by the Supplementary Benefits Commission' and where income tax is a *cause* of poverty.[309]

Frank Field draws attention to CPAG's proposals to raise the threshold and so make clawback more effective. He concludes, however, that it might be more desirable to revert to a fully universal benefit, in which 'even the articulate middle class would have a vested interest' (p. 157). Similarly, Sir John Walley would like to make a fresh start with a 'child endowment' scheme in which both family allowances and tax allowances would be replaced by a tax-free allowance. Another powerful advocate of such a scheme is Margaret Wynn. She presents a carefully argued case for a 'family policy' that would not divide the interest of families. Such a policy would have to avoid concentrating on the poor :

> If the objective of social policy is restricted to the elimination of poverty it is unlikely to succeed, because it must isolate the poor and fail to win the support of the majority of families, social policy should reflect the expectations of the majority of families and not only be concerned with the benevolent protection of the weak and needy.[310]

Mrs Wynn regrets the present political consensus on the need to concentrate family allowances on poorer families :

> The parties agree . . . in this essentially divisive approach which would never be supported by representative family organisation and does, of course, inhibit thought in terms of the genuine needs of families. The levels chosen for dividing the poor from the not-so-poor by all parties are also not technically defensible as levels reflecting a standard of living at all. The concepts would not survive negotiation with representative family organisations employing professionally trained negotiators armed with the facts on the standard of living enjoyed by families and by childless persons.[311]

In view of the opposition to family allowances that we have just examined, it may seem rather idealistic to think in terms of a family lobby for a benefit that recognises realistically the cost of rearing children. Yet a closer study of the 1957 survey results provides support for the argument that the present system of family allowances divides the interests of families. Almost half the families in the sample were ineligible for family allowances at the time of the survey and only three out of five had ever qualified.[312] Professional and managerial parents were much less likely to have found family allowances of help[313] and families with three or more children had derived much more help from them than had those with one or two children.[314] Commenting on the fact that almost a third of one-child families wanted less to be spent on family allowances, the report concluded that 'this reflects the unequal way families in the sample have benefited from them'.[315]

Viewed in this light, a more generous, tax-free family allowance payable to all dependent children must be an essential feature of a *family* policy. Yet the very success of clawback could make such a policy more unattainable. Clawback was an answer to the complaint that family allowances were being paid to those who do not need them; Margaret Wynn's case is that all families *need* help. Her book is a formidable demonstration of the cost of rearing children and she has little patience with the view that parents should be expected to meet these costs: 'the interests of the children are more important than parental pride or paternal status'.[316] This is a timely attack on parental smugness, but how little has changed since Eleanor Rathbone complained, in 1924, that 'a man has no right to want to keep half the world in purgatory, because he enjoys playing redeemer to his wife and children'![317]

Half the parliamentary candidates had encountered the objection that people should support their own children. Although only one candidate endorsed this view, it seems likely to be a particularly difficult one to overcome. Public opinion may no longer be hooked on the view that family allowances will influence the *quantity* of the population; but it is likely to take more than a world broadcast to convince people that they are essential to its *quality*.

Campaign against poverty

There remains a need for CPAG to restate and re-emphasise the case for family allowances. Yet although 'CPAG's main strength has been the agreement of its members to campaign around one key issue' (p. 149), it was apparent, even before the general election, that the Group needed other strings to its bow. The Conservative victory has made this even more necessary. If a Labour government had increased family allowances to the level demanded, the Group would have had to decide whether it was redundant; to stay in business in order to lobby for annual reviews; or to press for wider reforms that would do more to redistribute income in a way that we might expect of a Labour government.

Yet even if the Conservative Government had honoured its pledge to increase family allowances, the poor stood to suffer from some of its other promises. Quite apart from its interest in NIT, the Conservative Party's proposals for a shift towards indirect taxes and its hints of greater freedom of choice in health and welfare[318] did not augur well for the lower-paid. The subsequent announcement, in October 1970, of a new wave of selectivity, plus a FIS scheme which had not only the shortcomings of NIT but those of selectivity too, showed that CPAG would have a severe task under a Conservative government. It is a measure of the Group's disillusionment that it should publish, within ten months of the Conservative victory, a special issue of *Poverty*, devoted to 'Poor People and the Conservative Government'.[319]

Community action

While CPAG is rethinking its policy in the aftermath of Mr Heath's 'quiet and total revolution' (p. 154), some of its members, notably in the York branch,[320] are urging that any amount of revision of its strategies *for* the poor is not enough : the Group should be encouraging, and co-operating with, organisations *of* the poor. Richard Silburn illustrates some of the limitations of this proposal. Where, he asks, can the *communities* of poor people be found. The problems of poverty are among those problems

> which, no matter how heavily they may weigh upon a community are yet not of the community in a way which makes a local solution possible . . . To talk in terms of local solutions

in this situation is both misleading and misguided; indeed to encourage a search for local solutions could be positively harmful. (pp. 141-2).

Silburn goes on to discuss briefly a different type of *community* – as represented in the Claimants' Union. Inkeles has made the useful distinction between *ecological* (or *geographical*) communities, the members of which share a common area of residence, and *moral* (or *psychic*) communities, whose members share common interests.[321]

Discussion of community action is likely to be restricted too readily to ecological communities. But how does one identify such a community of poor people? The study of St Ann's revealed a range of incomes; the varying concepts of poverty; and a lack of a 'communalising experience', which underlined the futility of a search for a poor community. True, 36 per cent of the households were living in poverty – compared with the 14 per cent national figure of Abel-Smith and Townsend – and the authors reasonably claimed 'to have demonstrated . . . that poverty is concentrated into certain areas of a city, rather than being randomly distributed'.[322] But this hardly adds up to a community of poor people. Moreover, a third of the poor thought of themselves as 'comfortable' and only a seventh admitted to poverty.[323]

Silburn makes the useful comparison between community action as a strategy against poverty and as a reaction to slum clearance plans. Redevelopment is likely to be a 'communalising experience', in a way that poverty cannot be. At least, not in a geographical area. To expect residents of a given area to declare themselves 'poor' is 'both misguided and misleading'. It may be less stigmatising, however, to admit to the status of 'claimant', 'disabled', or 'unsupported mother'. Thus we have seen the emergence, in recent years, of the Claimants' Union, the Disablement Income Group and Mothers in Action.

The appearance of unity *within* such groups may be illusory: can we really expect 'deserving' supplementary pensioners to unite successfully with their unemployed counterparts, and 'respectable' widows to join forces with unmarried mothers? And if such alliances could be successfully formed, this would only accentuate the fragmented nature of this three-pronged attack on poverty. As it is, groups such as these present not only a divided front in the war on poverty but they may give us a false impression of the enemy. This is likely to be especially true of the Claimants' Union whose activities might cause people to believe that the war is to be waged against the Supplementary Benefits Commission; but all these groups could succeed in distracting 'attention from the wider question of wage and income redistribution, the real cause of poverty' (p. 142).

It will be up to the Child Poverty Action Group to concentrate attention, in the 1970s, on these wider issues, while helping to service client organisations with expert help and other assistance. Richard Bryant has urged that such a service should be one of CPAG's major roles;[324] and Robert Holman has concluded that pressure groups will have a continuing role, not only in servicing client organisations but in articulating the demands of the unorganised.[325]

Richard Silburn regrets the failure of the body which should have spoken for these groups: the Labour Party. The Labour Government vehemently denied CPAG's charge that 'low income families have not in fact been given priority in policy and in some respects they have even lost ground';[326] and many a CPAG activist will be able to recount being harangued, by the Party's faithful, for the Group's alleged contribution[327] to the 1970 election result. Yet subsequent publications, by Incomes Data Services Ltd, have confirmed that 'the differential between the higher paid groups and the lower paid groups is increasing' and that 'in some cases, those actually on the minimum are worse off now than they were two years ago or five years ago'.[328]

Mr Crossman has confessed that it would have been no good his proposing to 'bring everyone on to the supplementary benefit level' because 'the Chancellor [would not have dreamed] of letting it go'.[329] While one does not expect such candour from his colleagues, we must hope that the Labour Party, in opposition, will admit its failures and prepare itself for a whole-hearted attack on family poverty upon being returned to power. Or can the Conservatives, who have made such a calamitous start along the road to *A Better Tomorrow*, be persuaded to redeem their election pledges?

Our 'Programme for the Seventies' suggests how they might do so and thus provide a new deal for poor families in Britain.

Appendix

Assumptions relating to Table 2, p. 58, on Negative Income Tax

DAVID BARKER

As Atkinson points out,* the main difficulty of assessing the effects of NIT proposals by means of the data contained in *Circumstances of Families*, the report of the Ministry of Social Security's survey, is that information about gross earnings is not given. Yet these need to be known if hypothetical benefits under NIT are to be computed. On the other hand, the only alternative, the Inland Revenue Survey, is, as he concedes, scarcely more helpful for this purpose. Accordingly, I have endeavoured to use the Ministry's findings to calculate the relative effects of different schemes.

We know, from the Ministry's report, that 125,000 families with fathers in full-time work had resources below SB level (pp. 11-12). We also know the number of children in each of these. Tables II.5, A.8 and A.17 can be used to establish patterns of housing expenditure and the amount by which needs exceed resources; this profile can then be applied to the 125,000 families. The SB scale plus housing costs, derived from Table A.17, give the needs level against which net available resources are measured and income deficiency data enable us to compute the bands within which net resources lie. To obtain gross earnings (plus family allowances) it is then necessary to add to net resources the stoppages (National Insurance and graduated contributions, income tax and necessary working expenses) which

---

* References to the various publications mentioned in this appendix are given in the references, below, to Chapter 5.

had already been deducted to arrive at net resources. These gross earnings (with or without family allowances according to whether they are to be retained or abolished under the proposed NIT scheme) can then be used in conjunction with the tax threshold proposed under NIT to compute the NIT allowance payable.

To simplify the calculations, certain assumptions were made:

(a) all children were aged under 11 and therefore attracted, in 1967-68, a child tax allowance of £115 and a SB allowance of £1.25 or £1.50. The mean of £1.37½ was used in the calculations.

(b) a flat rate stoppage of £1 from gross earnings was made. This is probably an under-estimate and, to this extent, will *overstate* the allowance payable under NIT.

(c) November 1967 scale rates were used. This in turn presupposes that the overall pattern of available resources and housing expenditure of those below SB level in late 1967 or early 1968 was very similar to that prevailing in the summer of 1966 when the survey reported in *Circumstances of Families* was carried out.

(d) three bands of housing expenditure were adopted: under £2; £2 to £4; and over £4.

As an illustration both of the method used and of the reasons why NIT proves to be considerably less effective than its supporters claim, we can examine how various schemes affect a 2-child family with housing costs of £3. In November 1967, their SB scale needs were £12.80. Under assumption (b), their gross resources, therefore, were under £13.80 which includes a family allowance of £0.40. The effect of the £0.35 and the £0.50 family allowance increase will be to raise above scale 35 and 50 per cent, respectively, of those with a deficit of under £1 (assuming random distribution throughout this range). The remainder will still be below scale.

Under the IEA scheme, all will be brought up to scale, but no higher. Hayhoe retains existing family allowances, operates with a tax threshold of £14.10 and appears to favour a negative tax rate of 33⅓ per cent (i.e. one third of the gap between income and the tax threshold is plugged). Those at the upper limit (£13.80) will therefore receive a £0.10 NIT allowance and the allowance will increase by 5p for every £0.15 reduction in income. Only those with gross incomes of over £13.65 or 15 per cent of those with a deficit of under £1, will be brought up to or above scale under this scheme. Lees abolishes family allowances and makes up the deficit at the rate of £0.38¾ in the £. The abolition of family allowances means that those who were at the upper limit (£13.80) now have £13.40 and under Lees's proposals, with the tax threshold still at £14.10, they will receive £0.27 (i.e. their income will be cut by £0.13). Clearly no one in this category will be raised above scale by Lees's proposals; in fact, there will be a sizeable group whose family allowance had previously lifted them above the SB scale, who will now be below it. £3 is a fairly typical level of housing expenditure. If he makes the appropriate adjustments to the SB level, the reader will see how NIT favours those with lower housing costs and penalises those whose rent is higher.

Notes on contributors

David Barker. Lecturer in Social Administration, University of Manchester.

David Bull. Lecturer in Social Administration, University of Bristol. From 1969 to 1970, he was Chairman of the Child Poverty Action Group's Manchester and District Branch.

David Collard. Lecturer in Economics, University of Bristol. He has published work on several aspects of welfare economics and is the author of *Prices, Markets and Welfare* (Faber, forthcoming).

Frank Field. Director of the Child Poverty Action Group and Editor of *Poverty* since April 1969.

John Hughes. Vice Principal, Ruskin College, Oxford, where he lectures on economics and industrial relations. He is the author of many publications on trade unions and was a member of the TUC working party which reported, in 1970, on Low Pay.

Sheila Kay. Secretary of the Liverpool Personal Service Society. Formerly a lecturer in Social Science, a psychiatric social worker and Unit Organiser of the Liverpool and District Family Service Unit.

Tony Lynes. From August 1966 to March 1969 he was Secretary of the Child Poverty Action Group and Joint Editor of *Poverty*. He has written widely on pensions, family poverty and welfare rights.

Richard Silburn. Lecturer in Applied Social Science, University of Nottingham. Joint director of the survey of the St Ann's area of Nottingham.

Audrey Smith. Research student in the Department of Social Studies, University of Leeds.

Sir John Walley. Formerly Deputy Secretary of the Ministry of Pensions and National Insurance. Responsible for the preparation of the 1946 National Insurance Act. He had previously served in the Ministry of Labour from 1929. Since his retirement in 1966, he has written extensively on pensions, family allowances and means testing.

References and guides to further reading

All *Hansard* references are to House of Commons debates.

Introduction
1   A. B. Atkinson, *Poverty in Britain and the Reform of Social Security*, CUP, 1970.

Chapter 1: The rediscovery of family poverty
2   Brian Abel-Smith and Peter Townsend, *The Poor and the Poorest*, Bell, 1965, p. 30.
3   Labour Manifesto, 1950; reproduced in F. W. S. Craig, *British General Election Manifestos 1918-1966*, Political Reference Publications, pp. 127 and 132.
4   B. Seebohm Rowntree had conducted two earlier surveys of poverty in York, in 1899 and 1936: *Poverty: A Study of Town Life*, Macmillan, 1901; and *Poverty and Progress: A Second Social Survey of York*, Longmans, 1941. For an excellent summary of these, and other major poverty surveys before 1945, see D. Caradog Jones, *Social Surveys*, Hutchinson, n.d. A brief summary of inter-war poverty surveys is contained in PEP, 'Poverty Ten Years after Beveridge', *Planning*, Vol. XIX, No. 344, 4 August 1952, pp. 22-25.
5   B. Seebohm Rowntree and G. R. Lavers, *Poverty and the Welfare State*, Longmans, 1951, p. 40.
6   PEP, *op. cit.* (4), Appendix I, pp. 36-39.
7   Peter Townsend, 'Measuring Poverty', *British Journal of Sociology*, Vol. 5, No. 2, June 1954, pp. 130-137.
8   Ministry of Pensions and National Insurance, *National Insurance Retirement Pensions: Reasons given for Retiring or Continuing at Work*, HMSO, 1954, Table A1, p. 79. Subjective assessments of reasons for retiring should, however, be viewed with caution: for a critique of this, and other, surveys of reasons for retiring, see B. E. Shenfield, *Social Policies for Old Age*, Routledge, 1957, Ch. 3.
9   *Report of the Committee on the Economic and Financial Problems of Provision for Old Age* (Phillips Report), Cmnd. 9333, HMSO, 1954, para. 109.
10 See the 1953 and 1954 reports (Appendix III in each case) of the National Assistance Board, HMSO.
11 Phillips Report, *op. cit.* (9), paras. 213-14.
12 cf. n. 35 below.
13 Phillips Report, *op. cit.* (9), para. 262.

14   Peter Townsend, *The Family Life of Old People*, Routledge, 1957, p. 164; see also Penguin edition, 1963.

15   Dorothy Cole with John Utting, *The Economic Circumstances of Old People*, Codicote, 1962, p. 95.

16   Dorothy [Cole] Wedderburn ('A New Look at the Services Needed', in National Old People's Welfare Council, *Putting Planning into Practice*, 1966, p. 73) told the Thirteenth National Conference on the Care of the Elderly, in 1966, why her findings had been queried: 'We were told that the sample we used was too small and that it was not a national random sample. The reply I liked best of all was that nobody but the National Assistance Board could calculate entitlement to National Assistance'. She felt it was 'a crying shame that for four years we have argued about the facts which could have been checked [by the Government] right back in 1962'.

17   *Report of inquiry into the Impact of Rates on Households* (Allen Report), Cmnd. 2582, 1965.

18   Ministry of Pensions and National Insurance, *Financial and other Circumstances of Retirement Pensioners*, HMSO, 1966.

19   Peter Marris, *Widows and their Families*, Routledge, 1958, p. 129.

20   Audrey Harvey, *Casualties of the Welfare State*, Fabian Tract 321, 1960, pp. 8 and 31.

21   Howard Glennerster, *National Assistance: Service or Charity?*, Young Fabian Pamphlet 4, 1962.

22   Tony Lynes, *National Assistance and National Prosperity*, Codicote, 1962.

23   Dorothy Cole Wedderburn, 'Poverty in Britain Today – The Evidence', *Sociological Review*, Vol. 10, No. 3, November 1962, pp. 257-282.

24   Peter Townsend, 'The Meaning of Poverty', *British Journal of Sociology*, Vol. 8, No. 3, September 1962, pp. 210-227.

25   Tony Lynes, 'Poverty in the Welfare State', *Aspect*, August 1963, pp. 8-15.

26   Tony Lynes, 'A policy for family incomes', *The Listener*, 25 March 1965, p. 435-37.

27   CPAG, 'Family Poverty', *Case Conference*, Vol. 12, No. 10, April 1966, pp. 331-37.

28   MSS, *Circumstances of Families*, HMSO, 1967, Table II. 4, p. 11. See n. 168 below.

29   Vernon Bogdanor and Robert Skidelsky (eds.), *The Age of Affluence 1951-1964*, Macmillan, 1970, p. 7.

30   *Hansard*, Vol. 799, 15 April 1970, col. 1413.

31   *ibid.*, col. 1400.

32   The Conservatives (*A Better Tomorrow*, p. 23) promised to 'tackle the problem of family poverty and ensure that adequate family allowances go to those families that need them'; The Labour Party (*Now Britain's Strong – Let's Make It Great To Live In*, p. 20) undertook to 'review the present system of family allowances and income tax child allowances'; while the Liberals (*What a Life!*, p. 11) urged that 'the system of family benefits must be altered to include one-child families'. For a subsequent elucidation, by Mr Heath, of the Conservatives' pledge, see p. 153 above.

33   For discussions of income redistribution, see, for instance: A. T. Peacock (ed.), *Income Redistribution and Social Policy*, Cape, 1954; H. F. Lydall and J. B. Lansing, 'A Comparison of the Distribution of

Personal Income and Wealth in the United States and Great Britain', *American Economic Review*, No. 49, March 1959, pp. 43-67; H. F. Lydall, 'The Long-term Trend in the Size Distribution of Income', *Journal Royal Statistical Society*, series A, Vol. 122, No. 1, 1959, pp. 43-67; H. F. Lydall and D. G. Tipping, 'The Distribution of Personal Wealth in Britain', *Bulletin of the Oxford University Institute of Statistics*, Vol. 23, No. 1, February 1961, pp. 83-104; R. M. Titmuss, *Income Distribution and Social Change*, Allen and Unwin, 1962; C. Clark and G. Stuvel (eds.), *Income and Wealth*, Series X, Bowes, 1964; and J. L. Nicholson, *Re-distribution of Income in the United Kingdom in 1959, 1957, and 1953,* Bowes, 1965.
I am grateful to Ian Gough for providing these references. He modestly omitted to mention: I. R. Gough and T. Stark, 'Low Incomes in the United Kingdom, 1954, 1959, and 1963', *Manchester School*, June 1968, pp. 173-183.
Useful summaries of surveys of poverty have been cited already: *op. cit.* (4).
Three major articles on the definition of poverty have also been mentioned: Townsend, *op. cit.* (7) and (24); and Wedderburn, *op. cit.* (23). See also Peter Townsend (ed.), *The Concept of Poverty,* Heinemann, 1970.

Chapter 2: The failure of selectivity

34   The powers of local education authorities to assist with school uniform are to be distinguished from their powers to provide what is quaintly called 'necessitous clothing' to a child at a maintained or special school who 'is unable by reason of the inadequacy or unsuitability of his clothing to take full advantage of the education provided at the school': Education (Miscellaneous Provisions) Act, 1948, S.5(2). Most local authorities seem to operate this provision on the basis of a subjective interpretation of need rather than any defined criteria of entitlement. For the historical background, see Richard M. Titmuss, *Problems of Social Policy*, HMSO, 1950, pp. 118-20; 165-66; 374-76. In a recent enquiry, in Liverpool, into the knowledge of welfare benefits, three out of five respondents confused necessitous clothing grants with other benefits – usually school uniform grants: Peter Moss, *Welfare Rights Project Two,* Merseyside Child Poverty Action Group, 1970, pp. 4-5.

35   University students' grants differ from all the other benefits discussed in this chapter in that the problem of identifying those with low enough incomes to qualify is solved by paying a minimum grant of £50, regardless of income. For a salutary comparison between this generosity and the meanness of education maintenance allowances for children remaining at school after the statutory leaving age, see Mike Reddin, 'Local authority means-tested services', in *Social Services For All?*, Fabian Society, 1968, p. 13.

36   Cole with Utting, *op. cit.* (15).

37   Ministry of Pensions and National Insurance, *op. cit.* (18).

38   A. B. Atkinson, *op. cit.* (1).

39   Tony Lynes, 'Rate Rebates: What went wrong?' *Poverty,* No. 1, winter 1966, pp. 10-12.

40 The Minister of Housing promised 'to get the scheme more widely known, especially among tenants paying inclusive rents' (*Hansard*, vol. 760, 4 March 1968, Written Answers, col. 22). This category includes council tenants. In 1967-68, the percentages of council tenants and other indirect rate-payers who received rebate were 2.7 and 2.3 respectively, compared with 6.7 per cent of owner-occupiers and other direct rate-payers (*Rate Rebates in England and Wales 1967-68*, Cmnd. 3725, HMSO, 1968, p. 67). The fact that the 1968-69 figures were 2.7, 2.4 and 6.7 per cent, respectively (*Rate Rebates in England and Wales 1968-69*, HMSO, 1969, p. 66), while the 1969-70 percentages were 2.7, 2.4 and 6.8 (*Rate Rebates in England and Wales 1969-70*, HMSO, 1970, p. 65) suggests that the Minister's efforts had remarkably little effect.

41 *Hansard*, vol. 766, 21 June 1968, col. 1476.

42 For example, see *Hansard*, vol. 751, 27 October 1967, Written Answers, Cols. 577-78.

43 MSS, *op. cit.* (28).

44 *Poverty*, No. 4, autumn 1967, p. 17.

45 *Hansard*, vol. 738, 19 December 1966, Written Answers, Col. 202.

46 *Poverty*, No. 2, spring 1967, p. 3.

47 *Hansard*, vol. 749, 3 July 1967, Written Answers, col. 164; and vol. 807, 1 December 1970, Written Answers, col. 322.

48 MSS, *op. cit.* (28), p. 29.

49 For details of the package deal, see *Hansard*, vol. 751, 24 July 1967, cols. 56-66. See also Chapter 12 above.

50 'Health and Hardship', *Poverty*, No. 6, spring 1968, pp. 11-13.

51 'Prescription for Ignorance', *Poverty*, No. 8, autumn 1968, pp. 1-3. A subsequent survey, in 1969, showed that it was difficult or impossible to obtain, from a disturbing number of post offices, the appropriate form, as well as those for other welfare benefits: D. G. Bull, 'Out-of-form Post Offices', *Poverty*, No. 12/13, 1969, pp. 10-12.

52 *Hansard, op. cit.* (40), col. 7 and Written Answers, col. 3.

53 Judith Hart, 'Benefits are a Right', *Poverty*, No. 7, summer 1968, pp. 7-10.

54 *Hansard*, vol. 769, 25 July 1968, Written Answers, cols. 213 and 215.

55 *Hansard*, vol. 772, 4 November 1968, col. 462.

56 'The Disappearing Leaflet', *Poverty*, No. 10, spring 1969, pp. 15-16.

57 Mr Short, Labour's last Secretary of State for Education and Science, has revealed that his planned Education Act would have provided for a national system of education maintenance allowances: 'Edward Short's proposals for a New Education Act' (as related in conversation with the Editor), *Where*, No. 56, April, 1971, pp. 101-104.

58 For a discussion of some of the difficulties involved, see Tony Lynes, *Welfare Rights*, Fabian tract 395, 1969 (reproduced in Peter Townsend (ed.), *The Fifth Social Service*, Fabian Society, 1970); Rosalind Brooke, *Rights in the Welfare State*, Poverty pamphlet 4, CPAG, 1971; and Richard M. Titmuss, 'Welfare Rights, Law and Discretion', *Political Quarterly*, Vol. 42, No. 2, April-June 1971, pp. 113-132.

Chapter 3: Problems of accepting means-tested benefits

59 Mary Cooper, 'The Humiliations of Poverty', *Poverty*, No. 10, spring 1969, pp. 17-18.

60 Peter Moss, *op. cit.* (34).

61 Peter Moss, *Welfare Rights Project '68*, Merseyside CPAG, 1969.

62 This was despite the request from the Department of Education and Science, in its *Circular 12/67*, that local education authorities take steps to 'safeguard children taking free school meals from being identified'. Exposures by CPAG in Manchester, in November 1969, of continuing segregation (*Hansard*, Vol. 793, 11 December 1969, col. 617), are probably the 'recent events' mentioned in *Circular 4/70*, which called for a further effort to 'avoid embarrassment'. See also Chapter 2 above.

63 Dennis Marsden, *Mothers Alone: Poverty and the Fatherless Family*, Allen Lane, 1969. The quotations are from Marsden's summary in *New Society*, Vol. 13: 'Mothers Alone: Their Way of Life', No. 345, 8 May 1969, pp. 705-707; and 'Mothers Alone: The Wait for Help', No. 346, 15 May 1969, pp. 743-45.

64 MSS, *Administration of the Wage Stop*, HMSO, 1967, para. 18.

65 *Poverty*, No. 4, autumn 1967, p. 25; cf. p. 22 above. For further evidence of the low-paid worker's inferior use of his welfare rights, see MSS, *op. cit.* (28), paras. 67-69; and 'Health and Hardship', *op. cit.* (50).

66 John Barr, 'Durham's Murdered Villages', *New Society*, vol. 13, no. 340, 3 April 1969, pp. 523-5.

67 Family allowances were increased by £0.35 per child (excluding the first), in April 1968; but £0.25 of that increase was paid in respect of fourth and subsequent children, from October 1967. For details of these, and of a further increase in October 1968, see Chapters 10 and 11 above.

68 *Poverty*, No. 4, autumn, 1967, p. 13.

69 Working Party of the Liverpool Youth Organisations Committee, *Special But Not Separate*. A report on the situation of young coloured people in Liverpool, 1968, p. 8.

70 MSS, *op. cit.* (64), para. 21.

Further Reading

For further evidence of the humiliation endured by clients seeking means-tested, and other, financial help, see: Robert Holman, *Unsupported Mothers and the Care of their Children*, Mothers in Action, 1970; Robert Holman (ed.) (see n. 325 below); and John E. Mayer and Noel Timms, *The Client Speaks*, Routledge, 1970.

Chaper 4: The case for universal benefits

71 David Collard, *The New Right: A Critique*, Fabian Tract 387, 1968, Section 2.

72 Mike Reddin, *op. cit.* (35).

73 See Chapter 2 above for a discussion of the 1967 and 1970 campaigns to publicise, and improve the administration of, free school meals.

74 Some of the obstacles to the full uptake of free welfare foods are discussed in Chapter 2 above.

75 *Economic Trends*, No. 184, HMSO, February 1969, pp. xi-xxxix.

76 *Hansard*, Vol. 791, 17-18 November 1969, Written Answers, Cols. 210; 247-48.

N

77 See, for instance, Della Adam Nevitt, 'A National Housing Allowance Scheme', in *Social Services for All?, op. cit.* (35).
78 Allen Report, *op. cit.* (17).
79 R. H. S. Crossman, *Paying for the Social Services*, Fabian Tract 399, 1969, pp. 12; 21.
80 Collard, *op. cit.* (71), p. 15.

Chapter 5: Negative income tax
81 Milton Friedman, *Capitalism and Freedom*, Chicago, 1962.
82 *ibid*, p. 190.
83 *ibid*, pp. 191-192.
84 For a review of these, see Christopher Green, *Negative Taxes and the Poverty Problem*, Brookings Institution, 1967.
85 This is summarised by an IEA Study Group, *Policy for Poverty*, Research Monograph 20, IEA, 1970, pp. 51-56; and is more critically reviewed by Martin Rein and Ted Marmor, 'Nixon's Welfare Reform: a guaranteed minimum', *New Society*, vol. 15, no. 400, 28 May 1970, pp. 913-16.
86 Geoffrey Gibson, 'The Income Guarantee', *New Society*, vol. 4, no. 113, 26 November 1964, pp. 10-11.
87 CPAG, *op. cit.* (27).
88 Tony Lynes, 'Family Allowances in Great Britain', in Eveline M. Burns (ed.), *Children's Allowances and the Economic Welfare of Children*, Citizen's Committee for Children of New York, 1968.
89 Dennis Lees, 'Poor Families and Fiscal Reform', *Lloyds Bank Review*, October 1967, pp. 1-15.
90 Barney Hayhoe, *Must the Children Suffer?*, Conservative Political Centre, 1968.
91 IEA Study Group, *op. cit.* (85).
92 *ibid.*, p. 7.
93 C. V. Brown and D. A. Dawson, *Personal Taxation, Incentives and Tax Reform*, PEP, 1969, pp. 78-79; and The Open Group, *Social Reform in the Centrifugal Society*, New Society pamphlet, 1969, p. 24.
94 The idea was first put forward by Lady Rhys-Williams in *Something to look forward to*, Macdonald, 1943.
95 Brown and Dawson, *loc. cit.* (93).
96 *Hansard*, *loc. cit.* (31).
97 *Hansard*, Vol. 753, 8 November 1967, col. 1057.
98 *ibid.*, cols. 1092 ff.
99 Rosemary Marten, 'Negative Income Tax – The administrative problems', *Poverty*, No. 11, Summer 1969, pp. 9-11.
100 Conservative Party, *op. cit.* (32), p. 22.
101 DHSS, *National Superannuation and Social Insurance*, Cmnd. 3883, HMSO, 1969, para. 108.
102 In a CPAG survey of parliamentary candidates in the 1970 election, one in four favoured NIT as a way of tackling family poverty; but this included only one in nine Labour candidates. A majority, among Conservative and Labour candidates alike, preferred increased family allowances, while Liberals leaned towards a minimum wage: David Bull, 'Fresh Hope for the Poor?', *British Hospital Journal and Social Service Review*, 10 July 1970.
103 Douglas Houghton, *Paying for Social Services*, Occasional Paper 16, IEA, 1967.

104 *Hansard, op. cit.* (97), col. 1066; for details of R. M. Titmuss's 'universalist infrastructure', see his *Commitment to Welfare*, Allen and Unwin, 1968, pp. 122 and 135.
105 *Hansard, op. cit.* (97), cols. 1042 ff.
106 Crossman, *op. cit.* (79).
107 See Mr Macleod's exchange with Mr Taverne, *Hansard, op. cit.* (30), cols. 1412-13.
108 *Hansard, op. cit.* (97), cols. 1074 ff.
109 *Hansard*, Vol. 762, 2 April 1968, cols. 270 ff.; and Kenneth Guest, *Prescription for Poverty*, Scottish Liberal Party, 1968.
110 *Hansard*, Vol. 806, 10 November 1970, col. 294.
111 See, for example, Peter Kaim-Caudle, 'Selectivity in Family Allowances', in *Social Services for All?, op. cit.* (35); and A. R. Prest, *Social Benefits and Tax Rates*, Research Monograph 22, IEA, 1970.
112 Marten, *op. cit.* (99), pp. 9-10.
113 Atkinson, *op. cit.* (1).
114 DHSS, *op. cit.* (101); and Richard Titmuss, 'The practical case against the means-test state', *New Statesman*, 15 September 1969 (republished as 'Universal and Selective Social Services' in Titmuss, *op. cit.* (104), pp. 113-123).
115 IEA Study Group, *op. cit.* (85), p. 36, n. 3.
116 *Hansard, op. cit.* (49), col. 62.
117 Hayhoe, *op. cit.* (90), p. 16.
118 Lees, *op. cit.* (89), pp. 7-8; 12.
119 IEA Study Group, *op. cit.* (85), p. 48.
120 *ibid.*, p. 86.
121 Atkinson, *op. cit.* (1), pp. 130-184, especially 131-141, 151-169; see also pp. 29-43.
122 Brown and Dawson, *op. cit.* (93), pp. 52-68; Brown and Dawson explain more fully the income and substitution effects: p. 118.
123 See p. 124 above for an explanation of marginal tax rates.
124 Eleanor Rathbone, *The Disinherited Family*, Allen and Unwin, 1924.
125 Lees, *op. cit.* (89), pp. 2-3.
126 Hayhoe, *op. cit.* (90), pp. 16-18.
127 IEA Study Group, *op. cit.* (85), p. 24.
128 Lees, *op. cit.* (89), p. 5.
129 Open Group, *op. cit.* (93), p. 24.
130 Dennis Lees, *Health Through Choice*, Hobart Paper 14, IEA, 1962.
131 Arthur Seldon, *Pensions for Prosperity*, Hobart Paper 4, IEA, 1960; and *After the NHS*, Occasional Paper 21, IEA, 1968.
132 IEA Study Group, *op. cit.* (85), pp. 57-66.
133 Lord Balniel, in Hayhoe, *op. cit.* (90), p. 7.
134 See, for instance, Arthur Seldon's contention that universality 'appears to put equality before humanity . . . Yet even its equality is spurious, since equal treatment of people in unequal circumstances is inequality': 'Which Way to Welfare?', *Lloyds Bank Review*, October 1966, pp. 34-48.

Chapter 6: The family income supplement

135 In the 1970 Budget debate, Mr Macleod made clear his conversion to family allowances with clawback as a short-term solution to family poverty: *loc. cit.* (107). Although the Conservatives' promise, in their

manifesto – *loc. cit.* (32) – was couched in vague terms, Mr Heath confirmed, in a letter to CPAG (1 June, 1970), that his party stood by Mr Macleod's statement. For fuller details, see p. 153 above; and *Poverty*, No. 16/17, pp. 3-4 and 30.

136 *Family Income Supplements Bill*, HMSO, 1970.

137 *Hansard*, Vol. 814, 24 March 1971, Written Answers, Col. 146.

138 See p. 52 above.

139 *Hansard, op. cit.* (110), cols. 218-19.

140 *ibid.*, cols. 222 and 331.

141 *ibid.*, col. 257.

142 *Hansard*, vol. 805, 27 October 1970, cols. 50-51.

143 B. Abel-Smith, 'Poor Kids and Rich Kids', *New Statesman*, 6 November 1970, pp. 590-91.

144 H. A. Turner and F. Wilkinson, 'Real net incomes and the wage explosion', *New Society*, vol. 17, no. 439, 25 February 1971, pp. 309-10.

145 *Hansard, op. cit.* (110), col. 218.

146 The MSS, *op. cit.* (28), para. 40, calculated that there were 160,000 families in which the father was either in full-time work for a poverty wage or was wage-stopped. It was estimated that 25,000 of these were one-child families with a father in full-time work, but no estimate was given of how many of the 20,000 men who were wage-stopped had one child. Moreover, fatherless families were excluded from these figures. Comparison with Sir Keith Joseph's calculations for 1970 is, therefore, impossible.

147 *Hansard, op. cit.* (110), cols. 227-28.

148 Peter Townsend, *The Guardian*, 30 October, 1970.

149 See *Hansard, op. cit.* (110), col. 217, for the Secretary of State's apologetic reference to the quality of the information on which his estimates are constructed.

150 *ibid.*, cols. 256 and 285-86.

151 *ibid.*, col. 226.

152 *ibid.*, col. 227; see also the statement by Mr Peter Walker, the Secretary of State for the Environment: *Hansard*, vol. 805, 3 November 1970, cols. 852 ff.

153 *Hansard, op. cit.* (152), col. 853.

154 *Report of the Committee on the Rent Acts* (Francis Report), Cmnd. 4609, HMSO, 1971. Mr Julian Amery has announced the Government's acceptance of this recommendation made by the Committee: *The Guardian*, 11 March 1971.

155 *Sunday Times*, 8 November 1970.

156 See, for instance, Tony Lynes, 'Penalising the Poorer Tenant' *Poverty*, No. 8, autumn 1968, pp. 15-16; and Audrey Harvey, 'What help for poor tenants?', *Social Services for All?, op. cit.* (35). A comprehensive revelation of deficiencies in rent rebate administration is to be found in K. C. Mastin, *Rent Adjustment Schemes*, unpublished B.A. (Econ.) dissertation, University of Manchester, 1970.

True, the new scheme will be uniform and will be operated by large authorities. Experience of rate rebate administration suggests, however, that neither of these features is a guarantee of any drive to maximise uptake. See, for instance, Jennifer Dale, *Rate Rebates: Study of a Selective Scheme*, unpublished B.A. (Econ.) dissertation, University of Manchester, 1969; Lynes, *op. cit.* (39); 'Publicising Rate Rebates', *Poverty*, No. 8, autumn 1968, pp. 6-7; and Jonathan

Bradshaw and Malcolm Wicks, 'Where have all the rate rebates gone?' *Poverty*, No. 15, 1970, pp. 13-16.

157 Michael Zander comes to such a conclusion, as a result of his useful, small-scale study of the impact of the 1965 Rent Act: 'The Unused Rent Acts', *New Society*, vol. 12, no. 311, 12 September 1968, pp. 366-68. So too does David Donnison, 'How to help the Poorest Tenants?', *New Society*, vol. 13, no. 329, 16 January 1969, pp. 86-87.

158 *Hansard, op. cit.* (142), col. 41.

159 For an important analysis of how income tax bites below the supplementary benefit level, see David Piachaud, 'Poverty and Taxation', *Political Quarterly*, Vol. 42, No. 1, January-March 1971, pp. 31-44. The 1971 Budget changes in child tax allowances will have eased this problem: see p. 131 above.

160 Kaim-Caudle; and Prest, *op. cit.* (111).

161 *Hansard, op. cit.* (110), col. 225.

162 See, for example, the reply, during the Committee stage, of Mr Paul Dean, Minister of State for Social Services, to questions about the reason for the upper limit to the income supplement. 'A danger of abuse' and of 'collusion between a man and his employer' were said to be the reasons; it was 'not for reasons of cost': *Hansard*, vol. 806, 18 November 1970, cols. 1265-66.

163 *Hansard, op. cit.* (110), col. 265.

164 *ibid.*, col. 217.

165 *Hansard, loc. cit.* (31).

166 *Hansard, op. cit.* (110), col. 228.

Chapter 7: The role of family planning

167 For an understanding of some major studies indicating the importance of such variables as social class and education, see Clyde V. Kiser (ed.), *Research in Family Planning*, Princeton, 1962.

168 Ministry of Social Security, *loc. cit.* (28), Table 11.4 shows, for families of two or more children and with fathers in full-time work, the percentages of families of different sizes having resources below supplementary benefit level. While this proportion rose from 3 per cent of families with only two children to 21 per cent of those with 6 or more children, 64 per cent of families with inadequate resources had three children or less.

169 Ken Coates and Richard Silburn, *Poverty, deprivation and morale in a Nottingham Community: St. Ann's*, Nottingham University Department of Adult Education, 1967. Chapter 6 shows the low aspirations of the poor. For instance, 'wealth' is thought of as a weekly income, seldom in excess of £50 and, by almost a quarter of them, of no more than £25. Two out of five said they could live comfortably on their present income.

170 *ibid*, p. 21.

171 See Lee Rainwater, *And the Poor Get Children*, Chicago, 1960; and *Family Design*, Chicago, 1965, pp. 216-24. Rainwater suggests that lack of communication and understanding between spouses is one of the main obstacles to effective family planning, while sexual disharmony is another. Although the present study did not explore these issues in depth, their importance is apparent.

172 For a discussion of (a) the attitudes of low-income groups towards the use of coitus-connected (e.g. condom, cap) methods of birth control,

and sexual behaviour; and (b) how the role of oral contraceptives and the interuterine devices have made the question of birth control largely a social one, see Catherine Kohler Riessman, 'Birth Control, Culture and the Poor', *American Journal of Orthopsychiatry*, 1968, pp. 693-99.

173 Geoffrey Gorer, 'The Sunday Times Report on Sex and Marriage', Pt. 1, *Sunday Times*, 15 March 1970.

174 For a fuller discussion of the unpopularity, among this group, of male methods, compared with their popularity among the general population, see Hilary Land, *Large Families in London*, Bell, 1969, pp. 126-29. See also Griselda Rowntree and Rachel M. Pierce, 'Birth Control in Britain', Pt. 1: 'Attitudes and Practices Among Persons Married Since the First World War', *Population Studies*, Vol. XV, Pt. 1, July 1961; and Pt. 2: 'Contraceptive Methods Used by Couples Married in the Last Thirty Years', *Population Studies*, Vol. XV, Pt. 2, November 1961.

175 Ann Cartwright, 'General Practitioners and Family Planning', *Medical Officer*, No. 3130, 19 July 1968, pp. 43-46; and John Peel, 'Contraception and the Medical Profession', *Population Studies*, Vol. XVIII, Pt. 2, November, 1964.

176 Sir Theodore Fox, 'Family Planning', Nursing Mirror Conference Lecture, *Nursing Mirror*, 23 February 1968.

177 John Peel, 'Sociological Aspects of Contraceptive Usage', *British Journal of Clinical Practice*, Vol. 21, No. 6, June 1967; see especially Fig. 2, 'Class Composition of Clinic Patients', for a comparison of the 1927 clientele with that of 1960. See also François Lafitte, 'The Users of Birth Control Clinics', *Population Studies*, Vol. XVI, Pt. 1, July 1962.

178 See the reports on the Southampton and York schemes, respectively, in *Family Planning*, October 1964, p. 63, and October 1967, p. 68. The former is described also by Dorothy Morgan, 'The Acceptance by Problem Parents in Southampton of a Domiciliary Birth Control Service', *Medical Officer*, No. 2960, vol. CXIII, No. 16, 16 April 1965; and a five-year experiment in Newcastle-upon-Tyne is discussed by Mary Peberdy, 'Fertility Control for Problem Parents', *ibid*. See also 'Delivering Contraception', *World Medicine*, 3 June 1969, pp. 13-16; and John Peel and Faith Schenk, 'Domiciliary Birth Control: A New Dimension in Negative Eugenics', *Eugenics Review*, Vol. 57, No. 2, June 1965, pp. 67-71. The change of direction 'towards preventive work aimed at the younger "pre-problem" family' is recorded by the Family Planning Association, *39th report and accounts 1970-71*, p. 11.

179 FPA, *ibid.*, p. 3.

180 Labour's Secretary of State for Social Services argued that a lack of money, rather than of will, remained in 1970, the main obstacle to a free family planning service. On 9 March 1970, he assured the Commons that 'if we had unlimited money, there is nothing better that I should like to see than the principle of a free Health Service applied to family planning' (*Hansard*, Vol. 797, col. 889). The disappointing response by hard-up local authorities had helped to convince him that this service 'should be part of the National Health Service and provided for out of taxation'. Six weeks later, he was more reserved: while recognising the 'strong social arguments' for a

free service, 'notably the supply on prescription of free contraceptive pills', this raised 'large social and financial questions and [he had] no new policy to announce at present' (*Hansard*, Vol. 800, 30 April 1970, Written Answers, Col. 394). Although his Conservative successor has announced an increase in 'facilities throughout local government and hospital clinics for people who cannot afford the supplies involved' and has revealed the Government's belief 'that the principal growth in family planning should come in giving advice in the home to those who, for one reason or another, are not able to take advantage of contraceptive methods', he avoided answering directly even the modest request, from the Opposition spokesman on Social Services, that 'he consider making contraceptives available free of charge to those in need on social as well as medical grounds'. (*Hansard*, vol. 812, 23 February 1971, Cols. 313-18).

181 CPAG, *Poverty and the Labour Government*, Poverty leaflet 3, 1970.

182 CPAG, *op. cit.* (27).

183 For an airing of the differences, see Tony Lynes, 'Against Child Poverty', *Family Planning*, Vol. 15, No. 4, January 1967; and 'Letters', *Family Planning*, Vol. 16, Nos. 1-3, April; July; and October, 1967.

Further Reading

See various reports, in *Family Planning*, of the marriage surveys by Professor Glass of the Population Investigation Committee. The 1959-60 Survey is reported in the April 1963 issue. For some early results of a new marriage survey, see D. V. Glass, 'Contraception in Marriage', October 1968; and C. M. Langford, 'Birth Control Practice in Britain', January 1969.

For further work by John Peel, see 'The Hull Family Survey: I, The Survey Couples, 1966', *Journal of Biosocial Science*, Vol. 2, No. 1 January 1970, pp. 45-70; and his important book, with Malcolm Potts, *Textbook of Contraceptive Practice*, CUP, 1969. Other important reference books are: Elizabeth Draper, *Birth Control in the Modern World*, Allen and Unwin (cloth), Penguin (paper), 1965; and Jean Medawar and David Pyke (eds.), *Family Planning*, Penguin, 1971.

For further discussion of socio-psychological factors, see H. Lehfeldt and H. Guze, 'Psychological Factors in Contraceptive Failure', *Fertility and Sterility*, Vol. 17, No. 1, Jan-Feb 1966; E. W. Pohlman, *The Psychology of Birth Planning*, Schenkman, 1969; and Elizabeth Draper, 'The Social Background', in Mary Pollock (ed.), *Family Planning*, Balliere, Tindall and Cassell, 1966.

On unwanted pregnancies, see three articles in *Eugenics Quarterly*: Frederick Osborn, 'Excess and Unwanted Fertility', Vol. 10, No. 2, 1963; and E. W. Pohlman, (a) 'Results of Unwanted Conceptions: some hypotheses up for adoption', Vol. 12 No. I, 1965; and (b) 'Unwanted Conceptions: research on undesirable consequences', Vol. 14, No. 2, 1967.

For a discussion on the relationship between family poverty and family planning, see F. S. Jaffe, 'Family Planning and Poverty', in H. H. Meissner (ed.), *Poverty in the Affluent Society*, Harper & Row, 1966. On a wider front, see C. A. Valentine, *Culture and Poverty*, Chicago, 1968.

Chapter 8: Low pay: a case for a national minimum wage?

184 *Royal Commission on Trades Unions and Employers' Associations, 1965-1968,* (Donovan Report), Cmnd. 3623, HMSO, 1968, pp. 57-60; 65-68.

185 These are incorporated in the 1971 *Industrial Relations Bill,* HMSO, 1971, Part 9. They follow the lines suggested by the Donovan Commission. One important reform is to allow the assistance afforded by Section 8 of the 1959 Terms and Conditions of Employment Act to operate in the Wages Council sector. This means that Unions can seek from the Industrial Court an award where they consider that 'recognised terms and conditions' are not being observed by particular employers. The sting in the tail is that this procedure is available only to *registered* trade unions.

186 TUC, *Economic Review 1969,* pp. 32-36.

187 National Board for Prices and Incomes, Report No. 122, *Fourth General Report July 1968 to July 1969,* Cmnd. 4130, HMSO, 1970, p. 21.

188 For instance, Abel-Smith and Townsend, *op. cit.* (2).

189 TUC, *Low Pay,* TUC General Council Discussion Document, 1970.

190 In its *Economic Reviews* from 1968 to 1970, the TUC has been a powerful advocate not only of higher family allowances with tax allowances re-arranged to limit the benefits to those below the standard income tax rate, but also of the kind of re-organisation of income tax allowances to relieve the lowest income groups affected which was adopted in the 1970 Budget.

191 The most important source of information is the DEP's new survey of earnings in September 1968 which is published in the *Employment & Productivity Gazette* from May to October 1969. There is also information on pay dispersions in the Family Expenditure Surveys published each year; this material has the advantage of providing annual data from 1966.

192 See DEP, *A National Minimum Wage: An Enquiry,* HMSO, 1969. The criticism of the Working Party report is developed subsequently.

193 The earlier information on dispersion of earnings relates only to manual workers; it is published in the *Ministry of Labour Gazette,* April 1961.

194 Using the opportunity of reweighting expenditure provided by the Family Expenditure Surveys. It is relevant that the new official Index of retail prices for pensioner households shows a more rapid increase than the general index of retail prices.

195 See the table on p. 16 of *Low Pay, op. cit.* (189).

196 The material published in the *Employment & Productivity Gazette* for May and June 1969, which covers occupations and industries, uses only that part of the sample who worked a full week during the survey period. Anyone wishing to derive estimates of numbers of full-time workers from the sample must also examine the September 1969 *Gazette* which gives details of the full-time workers who lost some pay because they lost some hours of work in that particular week. Consequently, all the figures subsequently given involve estimation to include those other full-time workers.

197 It is interesting to note that, in September 1968, there were approximately as many men earning under £15 gross per week as were earning £40 and over. But for women workers there were approx-

imately 120 times as many earning under £15 as were earning £40 and over.
198 Quoted from DEP, *op. cit.* (192), p. 5.
199 *ibid.*, Ch. IV.
200 See *ibid.*, Ch. VI, cost assumptions of column A in the tables.
201 In September 1968, 16 per cent of manual men in 'all industries and services' earned less than £0.35 an hour (excluding overtime premia); but in agriculture, 78 per cent earned less than this an hour; in food manufacturing, 23 per cent; and in distribution, 31 per cent.
202 For 1967, an increase in household 'original' income from about £750 p.a. to £1,100 p.a. appears to have involved increased direct and indirect taxes accounting for 48 per cent of incremental income in the case of one person households; 37 per cent for two adult (non-retired) households; 32 per cent for households of two adults and one child; and 24 per cent for households of two adults and two children: *Economic Trends, op. cit.* (75).

Further Reading

The National Board for Prices and Incomes has directed a number of studies in low paid industries which have been more constructive than the conclusion reached in the *Fourth General Report, op. cit.* (187). These include: No. 29, *Pay and Conditions of Manual Workers in Local Authorities, the National Health Service, Gas and Water Supply,* Cmnd. 3230, HMSO, 1967; No. 48, *Charges, Costs and Wages in the Road Haulage Industry,* Cmnd. 3482, HMSO, 1967; No. 60, *Pay of Nurses and Midwives in the National Health Service,* Cmnd. 3585, HMSO, 1968; No. 101, *Pay of Workers in Agriculture in England and Wales,* Cmnd. 3911, HMSO, 1969; and No. 110, *Pay and Conditions in the Clothing Manufacturing Industries,* Cmnd. 4002, HMSO, 1969.

In May 1971, the Board published simultaneously three reports on low-paid industries and a general report on the problem: No. 166, *Pay and Conditions of Service of Ancillary Workers in the National Health Service,* Cmnd. 4644, HMSO; No 167, *The Pay and Conditions of Workers in the Laundry and Dry Cleaning Industry,* Cmnd. 4647, HMSO; No. 168, *Pay and Conditions in the Contract Cleaning Trade,* Cmnd. 4637, HMSO; and No. 169, *General Problems of Low Pay,* Cmnd. 4648, HMSO.

For a fuller discussion of wages councils, see the standard work by F. J. Bayliss, *British Wages Councils,* Blackwell, 1962. For a report on a local enquiry into their operation, see E. G. H. Armstrong 'Minimum Wages in a Fully Employed City', *British Journal of Industrial Relations,* Vol. 4, No. 1, March 1966, pp. 22-38. CPAG has published a list of the industries affected by wages councils, *Low Wage Employment,* Poverty leaflet 1, 1969. For comments on the problem of evasion, by employers, of these statutory minim see Adrian Sinfield and Fred Twine, 'The Working Poor', *Povert* No. 12/13, 1969, pp. 4-7.

Recent discussions of facts and policies on low pay includ Derek Robinson, 'Low Paid Workers and Incomes Poli *Bulletin of the Oxford University Institute of Economics Statistics,* Vol. 29, No. 1, February 1967, pp. 1-29; Ju Marquand, 'Which are the Lower Paid Workers?', *British Jou*

of Industrial Relations, Vol. 5, No. 3, November 1967, pp. 359-374; John Hughes, 'Low Pay and Incomes Policy', *Poverty,* No. 7, summer 1968; TUC, *Equal Pay,* Report of a Conference, November 1968; and John Edmonds and Giles Radice, *Low Pay,* Fabian Research Series 270, 1969 edition.

Chapter 9: Children's allowances: an economic and social necessity

203   *Congressional Quarterly,* 15 August 1969; and Sir John Walley, 'President Nixon's Family Allowances', *Poverty,* No. 12/13, 1969, pp. 15-17.

204   Dorothy Marshall, *The English Poor in the Eighteenth Century,* Routledge, 1926, p. 108.

205   A. E. Bland, P. A. Brown and R. H. Tawney, *English Economic History: Select Documents,* Bell, 1914, p. 655.

206   See, for example, G. M. Trevelyan, *English Social History,* Longmans, 1944, p. 469.

207   Bland *et. al., op. cit.* (205), p. 554.

208   *Social Insurance and Allied Services* (Beveridge Report), Cmnd. 6404, HMSO, 1942.

209   I know of no published source for this. My own reference has been to a photostat of the original made for the DHSS Library.

210   Similarly, I have no note of the source of my account of Pitt's income tax child allowances. I read of these in a history of the income tax in the Inland Revenue Library.

211   Bentley Gilbert, *The Evolution of National Insurance in Great Britain,* Michael Joseph, 1966.

212   Eleanor Rathbone, *op. cit.* (124); republished, with additions, including an epilogue by Lord Beveridge, as *Family Allowances,* Allen and Unwin, 1949.

213   *Report of the Royal Commission on the Coal Industry,* HMSO, 1925; see also *Family Allowances, op. cit.* (212), p. 255 and (for Beveridge's own account), p. 271.

214   Beveridge Report, *op. cit.* (208), para. 412.

215   'A Four Years' Plan', a Broadcast Survey of Post-War Reconstruction, 21 March 1943, in *War Speeches by the Rt. Hon. Winston S. Churchill,* compiled by Charles Eade, Cassell, 1944, vol. 4 *(Onwards to Victory),* p. 40; or see the definitive, 1952 edition, vol. 2, p. 432.

216   *Social Insurance,* Part I, Cmnd. 6550, HMSO, 1944, Para. 51.

217   In 1946, the allowances, for a family with three children, represented about 8 per cent of average industrial earnings. The October 1968 increase restored the figure to 8.2 per cent: CPAG, *op. cit.* (181), p. 18.

218   Alvin Schorr, *(a)* 'Income Maintenance and the Birth Rate', *Social Security Bulletin,* December 1965; and *(b)* 'Family Allowances and the Birth Rate', *Poverty,* No. 2, spring 1967, pp. 8-10; and Vincent H. Whitney, 'Fertility Trends in Children's Allowance Programs', in Eveline M. Burns (ed.), *op. cit.* (88).

219   Whitney, *ibid.*

220   *Hansard, loc. cit.* (49).

221   Beveridge Report, *op. cit.* (208), paras. 410-425.

222   The first part of the 1968 increase was announced on 24 July 1967, *Hansard, loc. cit.* (49), following the publication of the results of the

official enquiry into family poverty: MSS, *op. cit* (28). The second part was a feature of the government's attempt to counter the effects of its November 1967 devaluation. For fuller discussions, see Chapters 10 and 12 above; and CPAG, *op. cit.* (181), pp. 7-8.

223 There is a useful analysis in D. S. Lees's otherwise unhelpful discussion of proposals for a negative income tax, *op. cit* (89). See also Chapter 5 above.

224 First published in *The Times*, 11 December 1967.

225 TUC, *op. cit.* (186), p. 35; and *Economic Review 1970*, p. 59. For a brief account of the TUC's support for family allowances, see Hilary Land, 'Family Allowances and the Trade Unions', *Poverty*, No. 12/13, 1969, pp. 8-9.

Further Reading

The Conference report edited by Eveline M. Burns, contains much valuable information and discussion of various aspects of the subject including an essay, by Tony Lynes, on British family allowances, *op. cit.* (88). See also the postscript to this paper (n. 267 below).

For a powerful, up-to-date statement of the case for family allowances, see Margaret Wynn (n. 310 below).

Chapter 10: Clawback

226 J. M. Keynes, *How to Pay for the War*, Macmillan, 1940, p. 39.

227 CPAG, *op. cit.* (27).

228 C. N. Aydon, 'A new plan for child poverty', *New Society*, vol. 9, no. 225, 19 January 1967, pp. 93-4.

229 Memorandum to the Chancellor of the Exchequer, Supplement to *Poverty*, No. 2, spring 1967.

230 *Hansard*, Vol. 756, 16 January 1968, col. 1586.

231 *Hansard*, Vol. 756, 17 January 1968, cols. 1800-1.

232 'Mr Crossman and Social Services', *British Hospital Journal and Social Service Review*, 16 May 1969, p. 938.

233 *Hansard, loc. cit.* (31). Mr Macleod acknowledged, *Hansard, loc. cit.* (30), that this was a departure from his earlier condemnation (*Hansard*, Vol. 761, 20 March 1968, col. 437) of clawback.

234 Piachaud, *op. cit.* (159).

235 *Hansard, op. cit.* (110), col. 319.

Chapter 11:   The potential and limitations of community action

236 Coates and Silburn, (a) *op. cit.* (169); and (b) *Poverty: The Forgotten Englishmen*, Penguin, 1970.

237 Department of Education and Science, *Children and their Primary Schools*, a report of the Central Advisory Council for Education (England), (Plowden Report), HMSO, 1967. The report concluded that the disadvantages of children in deprived areas were so acute that a policy of 'positive discrimination', of additional expenditure upon the schools, was required to compensate for the environmental disadvantages. Thanks to the stringencies of government economic policy, only £16m has so far been allocated for this purpose, much of which will be spent on minor building works and bonuses for the teaching staff. More seriously, there is some considerable room for doubt as to what such expenditure can achieve, unless there are simultaneous

assaults on poor housing, low wages, and all the other aggravations that the poor endure. See the contributions by Ken Coates and Richard Silburn, and by Basil Bernstein, in David Rubinstein and Colin Stoneman (eds.), *Education for Democracy*, Penguin, 1970.

238 Colin Ward, 'Tenants Take Over', *Anarchy*, No. 83, January 1968.
239 See the pamphlet *Homelessness*, Solidarity, 1962.
240 Calouste Gulbenkian Foundation, *Community Work and Social Change*, Longmans, 1968.
241 Ministry of Housing and Local Government, *People and Planning*, Report of the Committee on Public Participation in Planning, HMSO, 1969.
242 Coates and Silburn, *op. cit.* (236), pp. 66-67.
243 Coates and Silburn, *op. cit.* (169), pp. 52 ff.
244 Ministry of Housing and Local Government, *The Deeplish Study: Improvement Possibilities in a District of Rochdale*, HMSO, 1966. See also the Denington Report, *Our Older Homes: A Call for Action*, HMSO, 1966. Both the Deeplish Study and the Denington Report argued that there were many thousands of houses which, while lacking many modern amenities, were none the less structurally sound. For a moderate cost, such houses could be brought up to modern standards, and would provide adequate and popular accommodation for several more years. The moderate costs would necessitate only moderate rents or repayments, and of course the physical and social disruption of comprehensive demolition and reconstruction would be avoided.

Further Reading

For a cautionary tale about some of the pitfalls that confront community action experiments, see Peter Marris and Martin Rein, *Dilemmas of Social Reform*, Routledge, 1967; and Daniel Moynihan, *Maximum Feasible Misunderstanding*, Collier-Macmillan, 1969.

A much more optimistic view, drawing mainly on varied British experiments is presented by Anne Lapping (ed.), *Community Action*, Fabian Tract 400, 1970.

For a brief critique of the Government's community development project, see Robert Holman, 'The Wrong Poverty Programme', *New Society*, vol. 13, no. 338, 20 March 1969, pp. 444-5. He develops this argument in his chapter in *Socially Deprived Families in Britain*, see n. 325 below.

A perusal of copies of the American journals, *Social Work* and *Trans-Action*, especially since 1965, will reveal a number of articles on specific community projects as well as on community action generally.

Chapter 12: A pressure group for the poor

245 For a flavour of the debate, see CPAG, *op. cit.*, pp. 22-31.
246 *ibid.*, p. 22.
247 CPAG, *op. cit.* (27), para. 14.
248 Abel-Smith and Townsend, *op. cit.* (2), pp. 39-41.
249 CPAG, *op. cit.* (229).
250 MSS, *op. cit.* (28).
251 For full details of the announcement and the ensuing parliamentary exchanges, see *Hansard, loc. cit.* (49).

252 CPAG, *op. cit.* (181).

253 For the original campaign leaflet, see 'Anti Wage-Stop Campaign', supplement to *Poverty*, No. 3, summer, 1967. For progress reports on the campaign, see *Poverty*, No. 3, pp. 12-13; No. 4, autumn 1967, pp. 6-7; and No. 6, spring 1968, pp. 6-7.
    The SBC's report – MSS, *op. cit.* (64) – published on 4 December 1967, was an important attempt to answer the recent 'considerable criticism' (para. 2) of the wage stop. In subsequent advertisements of its 'major successes', CPAG included the 'reform of the wage stop'.

254 CPAG, *The Wage Stop*, Poverty leaflet 2, 1969.

255 CPAG, *Guide to Supplementary Benefit Appeals*, Poverty leaflet 3, 1970.

256 For a preview of how the welfare lawyer's work might develop, see Rosalind Brooke, 'The Law and the Poor', *Poverty*, No. 10, spring 1969, pp. 7-9. Subsequent developments have included the establishment of a Citizen's Rights Office: see Audrey Harvey, *Poverty*, No. 15, 1970, pp. 17-18.

257 CPAG, *A Guide to National Welfare Benefits*, Poverty pamphlet 2, 1969. Some branches had helped in the publication of local guides, but a number had produced their own. The Merseyside branch participated in the production of the first local Welfare Benefits booklet (Liverpool Personal Service Society, 1968). York was the first branch to produce its own guide, in 1969.

258 For reports of the two Merseyside surveys, see Moss, *op. cit.* (34 and 61). For some of the findings see Chapter 3 above.

259 For instance, the York branch distributed leaflets on welfare benefits to 10,000 households: Jonathan Bradshaw and Richard Bryant, *Welfare Rights and Social Action: the York Experiment*, Poverty Pamphlet 6, CPAG, 1971.

260 Bradshaw and Bryant, *ibid.*, report on the York branch's weekly information stall in the local market. David Bull, *Action for Welfare Rights*, Fabian Research Series 286, 1970 – reproduced in Townsend, *op. cit.* (58) – describes CPAG's first experimental stall, opened by the Manchester branch in 1968. Both pamphlets discuss the value of such a strategy, and the dilemmas it creates, for an organisation that is campaigning for the substitution of more universal benefits for means-tested welfare benefits.

261 Bull, *ibid.*, p. 3.

262 W. J. M. Mackenzie, 'Pressure Groups in British Government', *British Journal of Sociology*, Vol. 6, No. 2, June 1955, pp. 133-48.

263 For an appraisal of the importance of trade unions in the campaign to establish family allowances, see Hilary Land, *op. cit.* (225).

264 This was the cost of increasing family allowances to £1.75 for each eligible child and 'clawing back' the increase from standard rate tax payers. For details, see CPAG, *op. cit.* (181), pp. 15-16.

265 *Hansard, loc. cit.* (230).

266 See Chapter 10 above.

267 See the postscript to a paper by Tony Lynes, *op. cit.* (88), which was reproduced for the CPAG conference on 'Family Poverty and Social Policy', 1969. The whole will be included in any publication of the proceedings.

268 CPAG, *Poor Families and the Election*, 1970.

269 Conservative Party, *loc. cit.* (32).

270   *Poverty*, No. 16/17, p.30.
271   David Butler and Michael Pinto-Duschinsky, *The British General Election of 1970*, Macmillan, 1971. Although the authors devote one whole page, out of 493, to pressure groups, CPAG was not one of the two mentioned.
272   *The Times*, 27 October 1970.
273   CPAG, *A Better Tomorrow for the Poor*, mimeographed memorandum presented to the Secretary of State for Social Services, September 1970.
274   *Hansard, op. cit.* (142), cols. 37-75.
275   *Hansard, loc. cit.* (152).
276   *Hansard, loc. cit.* (158).
277   R. A. Parker, 'Will we get a Fair Rents policy?', *New Statesman*, 20 November 1970, pp. 665-67.
278   *Hansard, op. cit.* (110), cols. 222-23.
279   See Chapter 6 above, and Frank Field, 'Poor People and the Conservative Government', *Poverty*, No. 16/17, pp. 3-17.
280   CPAG, *A Plan to Help Low Paid Workers and Overcome Family Poverty*, Memorandum presented to the Chancellor of the Exchequer, March 1971, reproduced in *Poverty*, No. 18, pp. 14-20.
281   See footnote to p. 113 above.

Conclusion

282   Peter Townsend, 'Introduction: does selectivity mean a nation divided?' in *Social Services for All, op. cit.* (35), p. 4.
283   Titmuss, *op. cit.* (104), p. 122.
284   David Donnison, 'Letters', *New Society*, Vol. 17, No. 437, 11 February 1971, pp. 246-47.
285   David Donnison, 'Taking your choice in welfare', *New Society*, Vol. 17, No. 433, 14 January 1971, pp. 61-62. The criticism is aimed at Ralph Harris and Arthur Seldon, whose book, *Choice in Welfare*, IEA, 1970, Donnison was reviewing. This particular charge is not taken up by Harris and Seldon in their 'Welfare: a rejoinder', *New Society*, Vol. 17, No. 436, 4 February 1971, p. 194; but Donnison restates his position even more strongly in his letter of 11 February: *op. cit.* (284).
286   Robert Pinker, 'The Contribution of the Social Scientist in Positive Discrimination Programmes', *Social and Economic Administration*, Vol. 2, No. 4, October 1968, pp. 227-41.
287   Sir John Walley, however, has argued that a means test involves a shift of tax even to those who *do* claim: 'Selectivity in the Social Services', *Social Service Quarterly*, Vol. 42, No. 2, September-November 1968, pp. 42-45.
288   See, for instance, IEA Study Group, *Towards a Welfare Society*, Occasional Paper 13, IEA, 1967, p. 7; and Harris and Seldon, *Choice in Welfare, op. cit.* (285), p. 5.
289   Arthur Seldon, 'Commitment to Welfare', Review Article, *Social and Economic Administration*, Vol. 2, No. 3, July 1968, pp. 196-200.
290   Arthur Seldon, *Taxation and Welfare*, IEA Research Monograph 14, 1967, p. 10.
291   Barbara Rodgers, 'A New Plan for Social Security', *New Society*, Vol. 12, No. 316, 17 October 1968, pp. 560-62.

292   See, for instance, *Hansard*, Vol. 781, 14 April 1969, cols. 767-74 and Written Answers, col. 200.

293   Bull, *op. cit.* (260), pp. 18-22. After a small door-to-door survey in Oxfordshire, Tony Lynes concluded that it might need 350 full-time civil servants to administer this sort of means-test advisory service; yet 'finding potential claimants is only half the battle. Getting them to claim, and holding their hands while they cope with endless application forms, is the other half – and much the more difficult and time consuming': 'Broadcasting Benefits', *New Society*, Vol. 16, No. 430, 24 December 1970, p. 1131.

294   John Baker and Christopher Cross, *The Newham Experiment*, mimeographed National Suggestions Centre, 1969; summarised in *What?*, summer 1969.

295   Balniel, *op. cit.* (133).

296   Hayhoe by Lord Balniel, *ibid.*; and Lees by Mr Tim Fortescue: *op. cit.* (98).

297   Moss, *op. cit.* (34), pp. 11-12; and Bull, *op. cit.* (102).

298   See, for instance, the 1969 report: DEP, *Family Expenditure Survey: Report for 1969*, HMSO 1970.
      This showed a steady increase, not only absolutely (pp. 12-13), but relatively (p. 74), in the expenditure on alcohol. Correcting all sums to the nearest penny, a weekly household expenditure of £1.13 (4.3%) on alcohol was the average for a range that stretched from £0.11 (1.2%) among households with an income under £6 to £3.11 (5.4%) for those with an income of £60 or more. True, the figures on drinking habits were among the most unreliable data collected in a survey which had only a 67 per cent response rate (p. 1, para. 5): they account for only about a half of the purchases that might be estimated from Customs and Excise statistics (p. 3, para. 14). Unless one argues, however, that the poor are the bigger liars (which is hardly consistent with their being the better co-operators in the survey: p. 2, para. 13), it is not possible to conclude that they are the greater spenders on alcohol; the contrary would appear to be the case.
      A weekly expenditure of £1.35 (1.5%) on smoking was the average for an interesting range. Absolutely, this rose fairly steadily from £0.34 to £2.37. The proportionate expenditure, however, reached a peak, of 5.9 per cent, in the £15 to £25 bracket.
      Data on gambling are not given in the main tables on household expenditure, but figures for 'betting payments *less* winnings' are among eight 'other payments recorded' (pp. 14-15). Both the absolute and relative relationships on income and betting expenditure fluctuated wildly.

299   Although the two pledges occurred in consecutive paragraphs of the Conservative manifesto – *op. cit.* (32) – it was quite clear that 'adequate family allowances' were not included in the promise of 'firm action to deal with abuse of the social security system'. This would entail 'tighten[ing] up the administration so as to prevent the whole system being brought into disrepute by the shirkers and the scroungers'.

300   See p. 25 above.

301   *Hansard*, Vol. 813, 10 March 1971, Written Answers, col. 127.

302 PEP, *Family Needs and the Social Services*, Allen and Unwin, 1961, p. 38.

303 Dorothy Wedderburn, 'How Adequate are our Cash Benefits?', *New Society*, Vol. 10, No. 263, 12 October 1967, pp. 512-16.

304 For a summary of IEA findings on this point, see IEA Study Group, *op. cit.* (288), pp. 32-33.

305 Mr Douglas Houghton and Mr David Ennals, respectively.

306 Crossman, *op. cit.* (79), p. 17.

307 Bull, *op. cit.* (102).

308 True, supporters of payments to fathers would not have to contend, in the House today, with Miss Eleanor Rathbone or Sir William Beveridge. See *Hansard*, Vol. 408, 8 March 1945, Cols. 2259-2370, especially 2275-83 and 2305-13.

309 Piachaud, *op. cit.* (159).

310 Margaret Wynn, *Family Policy*, Michael Joseph, 1970, p. 272.

311 *ibid.*, p. 264.

312 PEP, *op. cit.* (302), p. 189-90.

313 *ibid.*, pp. 67 and 158.

314 *ibid.*, p. 52.

315 *ibid.*, p. 193.

316 Wynn, *op. cit.* (310), p. 102.

317 Rathbone, *op. cit.* (212), p. 219.

318 Conservative Party, *op. cit.* (32), pp. 9 and 23.

319 *Poverty*, No. 16/17.

320 Cooper, *op. cit.* (59); Bradshaw and Bryant, *op. cit.* (259); and Richard Bryant, *Do the Poor Need Us?*, unpublished paper to CPAG Conference, 19 October 1969.

321 Alex Inkeles, *What is Sociology? An Introduction to the Discipline and the Profession*, Prentice-Hall, 1966, p. 69; quoted in Calouste Gulbenkian Foundation, *op. cit.* (240), pp. 2-3.

322 Coates and Silburn, *op. cit.* (169), pp. 53-54.

323 *ibid.*, p. 71.

324 Bryant, *op. cit.* (320).

325 Robert Holman (ed.), *Socially Deprived Families in Britain*, Bedford Square Press, 1970, p. 198.

326 CPAG, *op. cit.* (181), p. 10. The pamphlet, itself, includes two vehement retorts by Mr David Ennals: pp. 22-26 and 29-30.

327 cf. p. 153 above.

328 *Incomes Data*, Report 97, August 1970, pp. 23-29; and Report 98, September 1970, pp. 25-28.

329 *Hansard, op. cit.* (110), col. 253.

Index of Names

Subject Index

Abuse: 25, 27, 40, 81, 117, 152, 156, 162, 168, 189, 199
Agricultural subsidies: *see* Food subsidies
Application forms: 19, 23-25, 33, 39, 161, 184, 199
Attitudes: of earners to non-earners, 20; of family planning advisers, 84-85, 90; official to population question, 110; of parents to birth control, 10, 84-88, 92, 165, 189; of public, *see* Public opinion; of social workers, 134

Birth control: *see* Family planning

Charges: 4, 24-26, 39-40, 43, 74, 80, 90, 154-55, 158; *see also* School meals: price increase; Welfare foods: price increase
Child endowment: 114-17, 170
Child Poverty Action Group (CPAG): 145-47; advisory service, 31, 36, 149, 162, 197, 199; campaigns, 21, 145-47, 149-50, 152, 155-56, 171-72, 197; and clawback, 46, 72, 120-25, 148, 152, 168-69, 197; and community action, 36, 172, 174; and Conservatives, 152-55, 172, 188; and family allowances, *see* Family Allowances: and CPAG; and FPA, 92; and Labour, 145-50, 152-53, 169, 174; Manchester, 7, 185, 197; manifesto, 152; memoranda, 17, 120-24, 146-48, 155, 195, 198; Merseyside, 29n-30, 160, 183, 185, 197; minimum wage, 149; and NIT, 46, 52, 121; public education, 5, 145, 150; publications, 8-9, 24, 27, 34, 57, 172, 178, 182-98; surveys, 30, 149, 167-69, 171, 183, 186, 197, 199; and wage stop, 197; and welfare benefits, 22, 25, 26, 29n-30, 149, 183, 197, 199; and welfare law, 149; York, 172, 197
Child tax allowances: *see* Income tax: child allowances
Children's Allowances: *see* Family Allowances
Children's Department: 35
Claim, Claiming: conditions for, 24, 26-27, 30, 34; costs of, 9, 39, 198; deterrents to 23, 39,

161; encouragement to, 21, 24-26, 199; failure to, 21-23, 29-32, 35, 40, 79, 149, 161; fraudulent, *see* Abuse
Claimants: *see* National Assistance: households drawing: Selective Benefits: claimants; Supplementary Benefits: claimants
Claimants' Union: 142, 173-74
Clawback: 7, 11, 18, 46, 50, 64, 70-73, 81-82, 112, 114, 118-33, 148, 151-53, 155, 164, 168-71, 187, 195, 197
Clothing, necessitous: 30, 39, 183
Collective bargaining: 10, 93-94, 103-4, 166
Community: action, 7, 11, 134-44, 172-73, 196; associations, 34, 136-37, 140-44; development, 4, 135, 196; of the poor, 134, 172-73; sense of, 2, 137-42, 173; work, 142-43
Conservative Party, Government: abuse, 81, 168, 199; charges, 26, 154-55, 158; CPAG, 172, 188; clawback, 18, 70, 128, 132, 187-88, 195; election victory, 1970, 9, 70, 153-54, 172; family allowances, 3, 18, 47, 70, 82, 110, 128, 152-55, 163, 168, 172, 182, 186-88, 199; family planning, 191; FIS, 9-10, 70, 77, 82, 128, 172; housing, 76, 79, 154, 188; inequality, 153; manifestoes, 48, 152-53, 182, 188, 199; minimum wage, 101; NIT, 47-49, 162, 172, 186; poverty, 76-77, 80-81, 128, 152-54, 182; public expenditure, 163-64; Research Department, 48; selectivity, 172; Social Security, 48, 75, 182; social strategy, 76, 163; spokesmen, 48, 128; tax, 164, 172
Contraception: *see* Family planning; methods, 83-84, 86-91, 189-91
Council housing: 41, 45; tenants, 21, 41, 79, 159, 184

Deflation: 147-48, 151, 153
Devaluation: 4, 125, 148, 151, 168, 195
Disablement: 38, 49, 107, 115, 158, 173; benefits, 4, 109
Disablement Income Group (DIG): 52, 173